PUNISHMENT
the
supposed justifications

Punishment

the supposed justifications

TED HONDERICH

HUTCHINSON OF LONDON

HUTCHINSON & CO *(Publishers)* LTD
178–202 Great Portland Street, London W1

London Melbourne Sydney
Auckland Bombay Toronto
Johannesburg New York

★

First published 1969

© Ted Honderich 1969

*This book has been set in Baskerville, printed in Great Britain
on Antique Wove paper by Anchor Press, and
bound by Wm. Brendon, both of Tiptree, Essex*

09 096900 6

For Pauline, Kiaran, Rooney

Contents

CHAPTER 5 COMPROMISES

CHAPTER 6 LIBERTY AND PUNISHMENT

Preface

This book is given over to the analysis and assessment of arguments. It has been my intention to consider all that I find intelligible and at all persuasive by way of defences of the practice of punishment, and also to pay some attention to persistent obscurities. I have, necessarily, found myself dealing with the several large moralities which come into clear conflict over punishment and may, indeed, be appraised by way of it. I have also, necessarily, dealt with subject-matters that require for their most satisfactory handling something other than philosophical expertise. Here, there is the statistician's question of the efficacy of punishment as a deterrent, the many questions of a factual character about conceptions of criminality as disability or disorder, the jurisprudent's questions about strict liability in the law. Responses to the question of why we punish, where that is not the question of what reasons we can give, are no part of my concern. The first three chapters deal with traditional 'theories of punishment', for themselves and also because they emerge in contemporary doctrines. The fourth chapter is about human freedom and responsibility and their relevance to punishment. The fifth chapter is concerned with the contemporary doctrines just mentioned, the sixth with the general question of what behaviour of individuals should lie beyond the reach of the law. I am especially indebted to Professor H. L. A. Hart, whose writings have contributed a great deal, and to Professors P. H. Nowell-Smith and Richard Wollheim. I wish also to thank especially Professor Patrick Corbett, whose idea it was that the book should be written.

I

Retribution

1. *Description*

PUNISHMENT is not treatment, although offenders and also some patients are subjected to deprivation or distress. Anything we describe as punishment must involve some such thing, which, indeed, is one of its aims. This remains true, although the aim is not the end, when punishment is imposed as a deterrent and thought to be justified as such. Treatment, obviously, has no such aim but rather seeks to avoid distress whenever possible. It mostly does. Punishment, secondly, is not revenge, although certain of its supposed justifications would go some way to justifying revenge and some of those who punish share motivations and needs with those who take revenge. A man who has been injured by another and then revenges himself upon him is not *authorised* to act as he does. That is, he is not empowered by generally accepted rules, as a judge is empowered by the law, to fix and enforce penalties. If there are practices governed by generally accepted rules, where the injured man or his family exacts the penalty, these approach to being practices of punishment. Punishment is not, still more obviously, something done to a man chosen at random and without regard to his previous conduct. Punishment, or so we habitually think, is imposed on an offender, someone who is found to have broken a rule, to have done something prohibited. It may then seem, given these rudimentary differentiations, to be *an authority's infliction of a penalty*, something unwanted, *on an offender*, someone found to have broken a rule, *for an offence*, an act of the kind prohibited by the rule.

Is this description true of all practices which we are ordinarily willing to call practices of punishment? (A practice is to be understood as a set of actions, rule-governed or at least of a persistent character or aim.) If our description is too restrictive, this is so partly for the reason that not all punishments take place within a society's ordinary legal and penal systems. It may be said that punishments are not always the work of the authorities, persons or groups of persons empowered to act by rules that have something like a general acceptance. 'War criminals' are said to be punished despite doubts as to whether the tribunals of the winning side count as authorities. It may also be denied that punishment is always preceded by an offence, assuming an offence to be an action that goes against a rule previously stipulated. Certainly a father is unlikely to have announced, before his son does some astonishing thing, that no one was to do *that*. Perhaps he may be taken as having announced something so general as that his son wasn't to behave in outrageous ways. Might there be similar cases which we would call cases of punishment and where the point was to teach a quite new rule? If there are such cases, where there have not been offences, are these also cases where the person punished is not an offender, someone found to have broken a rule? They necessarily are, given the understanding we shall adopt of what it is to find that someone has broken a rule. We shall take finding in this context to be like knowing, so that what is found must be true. Furthermore, to find that someone has broken a rule is to decide in good faith, and by way of certain procedures, that he has broken it. A judge cannot find someone to have broken the law, in this sense, if he is convinced that he hasn't done so. Nor can he find him to have broken the law if he does not investigate the matter in certain ways.

It may also be suggested on the basis of quite different examples that punishment is not always of an offender. We speak of collective punishments of groups, such as classes in schools and villages in wars, some only of whose members have offended. More importantly, in English and American law, a shopkeeper who sells adulterated food, without intending to do so and without having been careless, may none the less be penalised. So may a motorist who without being negligent runs into a pedestrian under certain circumstances. An English publican who sells whisky to an intoxicated man, without knowing the man's state or being careless about finding out, is in the same position. It is also an offence under certain circumstances to seduce a girl under sixteen, and remains one if the man made an honest mistake in thinking she was older. That he did not intend to break the law is not a defence. These are offences of 'strict liability', which are not now a merely peripheral part of the law and may be more pervasive in the future. There is also 'vicarious liability'. A shop owner may be responsible if his clerk sells adulterated food. The owner of an English theatre could until recently be successfully prosecuted if without his knowledge or carelessness a play was presented which contravened the censorship rules of the Lord Chamberlain. Employers generally may be responsible for certain acts of their employees. Surely, it may be said, none of these could be regarded as offenders in the given sense.

What difficulties do these cases raise for our informal definition of punishment? Do they show we have not captured the ordinary notion of punishment? They are put forward as instances of punishment, instances of what we would ordinarily regard as punishment, and also as instances where some feature specified in the given description is missing. On further reflection, most people may be inclined to say of several of the cases either that they *do* possess the feature in question and *are* punishments, or that they lack it and should not be regarded as punishments. What is done to 'war criminals' may be taken to be punishment by those who accept that the tribunals count as authorities. Those who do not accept this will give some other description to the practice, or to particular instances of it. So perhaps with the father-and-son case. If it is accepted that there was *no* antecedent rule of a relevant character it will go against the grain to call the case one of punishment. One can deal in a related way, perhaps, with 'collective punishments'. Strict and vicarious liability present the real difficulty. Some people may be ready to name as punishment what is done in such cases, perhaps out of a kind of determined orthodoxy. Others will not be willing to regard what is done as punishment. Fortunately, we need not decide on the most common tendency. What we want is a description of punishment convenient for our purposes. It must certainly be in line with the ordinary understanding of the term, but over cases where there is no agreement, or where any existing agreement is not obvious, we may make our own decisions. Nothing of a substantial nature follows from this with respect to the main question we shall be considering. It will be convenient to take up a description or informal definition which allows us to use the term 'punishment' of cases of strict and vicarious liability. The description we have, however, where punishment is *an authority's infliction of a penalty on an offender for an offence*, does not allow this.

Suppose we take it to be established that a man's action in selling adulterated food in no way resulted from a relevant intention of his or any carelessness. There is a sense, or perhaps it would be preferable to say that there are contexts of discussion, in which it would be mistaken to say that he *broke a rule* and hence was an offender as so far defined. It would be mistaken to say this in a context, certainly an ordinary one, where it would be taken to imply that he was at fault or responsible, in ordinary meanings of those words. On the other hand, there is a sense in which he did break a rule. After all, one can break a rule unknowingly. The man, then, may be understood to have broken a rule although not to have done so with intention or negligence. Vicarious liability is another matter. One could not without absurdity exhibit the theatre owner or unfortunate employers generally as individuals who have broken rules.

The description as it stands has another quite different disability. It specifies that punishment is *for an offence* and so may be taken to imply that the moral justification of punishing a man is that he deserves it for what he has done. If we were to use this description, it might appear that we had so described punishment that the question I wish to ask, 'What, if anything, justifies it morally?', was already answered by the description. The answer might appear to be built-in and anyone who

disputes it, or anyone else for that matter, might protest that
the outcome of the inquiry could hardly be in doubt. Is there
anything to be said *for* the inclusion of the words 'for an offence'?
The description containing them may be regarded as having
significance in two ways. It specifies certain necessary features
of anything we shall count as punishment, of which one is that
a man must be found to have committed an offence, and it also
may be taken to suggest an *attitude* to this feature. In stating
that the penalty is *for* the offence, as we have seen, it may be
taken to suggest that punishing a man is justified because he
deserves it for the offence. This attitude is not itself a necessary
feature of what we shall take to be punishment. We shall not
regard something as other than punishment if a judge, supposing him to be the relevant person, does *not* hold the view that
the penalty he imposes is morally justified because it is deserved.
We shall not be bothered if, through a certain mistaken
enlightenment, he takes the view that the existence of an offence
is important in *only* another way: merely as an indication that
the man is one who is likely to offend in the future if he is not
deterred. This is a consideration in favour of excluding from
our description the words 'for an offence'.

Given this, and the difficulties raised by strict and vicarious
liability, let us describe punishment as simply *an authority's
infliction of a penalty on an offender,* and allow an offender to
be a man who has broken a rule, out of intention or negligence,
or a man who has broken certain rules out of neither, or a man
who occupies a certain position of authority with respect to a
rule-breaker in either of the preceding senses. There is no need,
I think, to be more specific about the mentioned positions of
authority, which have to do with cases of vicarious liability.[1]
They are in the main positions had by employers legally
responsible for certain acts of their employees.

Our description, so interpreted, is reasonably satisfactory for
our purposes. Perhaps, despite what I have said, it does not fit
everything that is ordinarily called punishment, whether by

1. For accounts of strict and vicarious liability see Glanville Williams,
Criminal Law, The General Part, Second Edition (London, 1961), Chapters
Six and Seven.

parents, teachers or irregular tribunals. It does fit the subject in hand: one of the dominant practices of control within democratic societies. The authorities in question are, in England, the magistrates and judges of the Magistrates' Courts, Quarter Sessions, Assize Courts, the Court of Criminal Appeal and the House of Lords. The offenders are most[2] of those found to be legally responsible with respect to offences. The latter are crimes of violence to persons, including murder and assault, crimes involving the property of others, including theft and damage, crimes gathered under the heading of 'nuisance', crimes consisting of certain acts considered to be immoral, and finally certain crimes against the state and some of its institutions, including treason and the subversion of justice. The penalties are those fixed by law. In the main, the law sets down maximum penalties for offences. The choice in a particular case, fine or imprisonment or worse, is made by the magistrate or judge.[3]

If the given description is suitable for our purposes, it is also true that it departs from most or all of the many definitions provided by philosophers who have considered the question of punishment.[4] This is so for several reasons, one of them that almost all philosophers have attempted to capture the (or *a*)

2. Having defined 'offenders' partly as those who *have* broken rules, not all of those individuals who are found guilty, and who thus are offenders in a strictly legal sense, are offenders in our sense. Judges make mistakes. Our definition has this inconvenience and avoids greater ones.

3. The offences, penalties, principles and practices of English law are concisely surveyed in P. J. Fitzgerald, *Criminal Law and Punishment* (Oxford, 1962).

4. Philosophers have given a good deal of attention to the definition of punishment, partly because some arguments about its justification have been supposed to rest on how it is defined. Antony Flew, '"The Justification of Punishment"', *Philosophy*, 1954; A. M. Quinton, 'On Punishment', *Analysis*, 1954; K. Baier, 'Is Punishment Retributive?', *Analysis*, 1955; John Rawls, 'Two Concepts of Rules', *Philosophical Review*, 1955; H. L. A. Hart 'Prolegomenon to the Principles of Punishment', *Proceedings of the Aristotelian Society*, 1959–60; K. G. Armstrong, 'The Retributivist Hits Back', *Mind*, 1961; H. J. McCloskey, 'The Complexity of the Concepts of Punishment', *Philosophy*, 1962; Thomas McPherson, 'Punishment: Definition and Justification', *Analysis*, 1967.

common or ordinary notion. Most people do have the feeling that at least part of the justification of punishment is that it is deserved, and this attitude finds expression in their use of the term. Some such implication is thus present in most definitions. Also, of course, given this genesis of definitions in ordinary life, and a want of awareness there of the existence of strict and vicarious liability, the definitions have excluded a part of their intended subject-matter. This has issued, if not in clear mistakes, at least in an overlooking of things of relevance. Finally, let me admit what will be obvious to some, that I have by some comparisons[5] been casual in formulating my description. It has been safe to assume, I hope, that readers do not need reminding by explicit clause that punishment is not a matter of fortuitous misfortune. There would be better reason for demanding a fuller specification of, say, the nature of the authority involved. What has been said seems to me sufficient for the arguments I intend to consider and to put forward.

2. *Problem and Answers*

The problem of punishment arises mainly but not only for the reason that the practice involves what traditionally has been called suffering. It involves a deliberate and avoidable infliction of suffering, a work of men. (It has sometimes been suggested[6] that it is in part an automatic reflex of society, like that of a living body to injury. This is at best darkening metaphor, and any suggestion that punishment is wholly an ungoverned reaction would be absurd.) It is certainly true that by comparison with penalties visited on offenders in the past,

5. '... a person is said to suffer punishment whenever he is legally deprived of some of the normal rights of a citizen on the ground that he has violated a rule of law, the violation having been established by trial according to the due process of law, provided that the deprivation is carried out by the recognised legal authorities of the state, that the rule of law clearly specifies both the offence and the attached penalty, that the courts construe statutes strictly, and that the statute was on the books prior to the time of the offence'. Rawls, *op. cit.*, p.10.

6. Recently by Ernest Barker, *Principles of Social and Political Theory* (Oxford, 1951), p.182.

B

many of our present penalties are humane. Is it then inappropriate to describe contemporary penalties as giving rise to suffering? 'Most punishments nowadays are not afflictions of suffering,' we are told, 'either physical or mental. They are the deprivation of a good. . . . Imprisonment and fine are deprivations of liberty and property. The death sentence is deprivation of life; and in this extreme case every attempt is made to exclude suffering. . . . We have taken the . . . important step of substituting the removal of something desired for the infliction of positive suffering.'[7] This less than reassuring distinction between deprivation and afflictions of suffering need not detain us. What is unlikely to be disputed is that penalties now imposed on offenders, whether or not they are to be described as causing suffering, do raise a question of moral justification. For one thing, more is now known of their destructive consequences, both on the offender and on others related to him. The question would correctly be raised, however, even by a practice which did no more than deprive a man of his usual liberty, or his usual resources, in some exceedingly sensitive fashion. The moral question arises, secondly, with respect to any system of punishment, as a consequence of a different fact: that others than those punished are coerced by it. One need not, in order to regard this as a consideration of importance, believe the laws in question to be bad ones. Thirdly, and vaguely, it can hardly be denied that the quality of life in a society, the quality of its public and private institutions and relationships, is influenced by the existence of a central practice of an authoritarian and repressive nature.

This claim, that one cannot but regard punishment as in need of justification, is itself a judgement of a moral nature. Like many to follow, it is an integral part of this inquiry. What cannot also be a part is the general problem of the nature of such judgements and the support they can have. I shall adduce no general arguments about their validity or invalidity. However, although the subject is one of complication and difficulty, I see no reason quickly to admit that what will be said here is a

7. J. D. Mabbott, 'Professor Flew on Punishment', *Philosophy*, 1955, pp. 257–8.

consequence of 'subjective responses' or 'individual moral attitudes'. It seems an arguable proposition, if not about men then about many men, that their impartial evaluations of actions begin from two fundamental attitudes, one having to do with securing human welfare and avoiding its contraries, the other with the distribution of welfare and its contraries. If this is the origin of particular evaluations, they are none the less often inconsistent with it. Often when they are regarded as logical consequences, they are not this. Between origin and particular conclusions come consideration of facts, imagination, and operations of derivation. Each of these allows, to say the least, for error. It is a work of practical, philosophical reflection to clarify judgements, to test them for consistency with others and with fundamental principles. Given the assumption that we share such fundamental attitudes, anyone who feels that he has arrived at true consequences of them, however novel, will take the view that these consequences are not peculiarly his own.

In the past, single reasons have often been given for the rightness of punishment. One of these reasons, which may be expressed with deceptive simplicity, as it already has been above, is that punishment is deserved by offenders. This is retributivism. Another claim, historically associated with utilitarianism, is that punishment serves to deter others from offending. We are usually too simply told that men are made fearful of breaking the law or that they keep it out of a prudent awareness of the possibility of punishment. A third claim is partly that punishment, or a practice of treatment, secures that fewer offences will be committed in the future, but not through deterrence. It was once the case, but is no longer, that all views of this third kind could be positively described as recommending the 'moral regeneration' of individuals as an end in itself and also a means to the prevention of crime. These three claims, each with variants and complexities, have been known as *theories* of the justification of punishment. This is so, perhaps, partly because it has been assumed that punishment or some closely related practice is an indubitable social necessity. Given this seeming fact, what is to be done is to provide a hypothesis or theory in explanation, as one provides theories about facts of the physical world. I shall keep the usage for its usefulness, not for this implication.

More recently, philosophers and others have contended that none of these three reasons taken by itself is sufficient to justify punishment or related practices of enforced treatment. Two or even more are needed in combination. Sometimes a number of reasons are mentioned but one is accorded a very secondary importance. We are told that the traditional retribution theory is correct since punishent is justified because it is deserved, and then reminded that punishment also has the recommendation that it deters. It may be that these are no more than the standard compromises just mentioned, variously disguised in an attempt to keep an old flag flying.

In order to clarify what is involved in each of the three original claims and their later unions, I shall begin by looking at them separately. That is, I shall consider each one as historically it was regarded, and in several cases still is, as sufficient by itself to show the rightness of punishment. This procedure will have the advantage of demonstrating why it has been thought that no single claim is sufficient. More important, as I have said, it may bring into clarity the elements of the ensuing compromises.

One other preliminary point. The inquiry in hand is in a certain sense theoretical. Supporters of the deterrence theory are not committed *by their theory* to the support of any existent practice of punishment. They are committed only to the support of any practice which *does* satisfy requirements which they stipulate. They are unlikely to have the detailed factual knowledge about, say, punishment in England or the United States which would enable them to make authoritative judgements on the actual state of things. They may be undeterred by this (as others with a greater factual awareness are undeterred by a lack of examined principles). None the less, whatever their factual knowledge, their theory does not by itself dictate such judgements. Precisely the same is true of retributivism and the other mentioned doctrines. What is also true, of course, as I have implied, is that theory clearly is a prerequisite of judgement.

3. *Traditional Retributivism*

One of the most influential statements of the retribution theory was given by Immanuel Kant in the eighteenth century. The following passages, central if not entirely lucid, are from his *Philosophy of Law*.[8]

... Punishment can never be administered merely as a means for promoting another Good, either with regard to the Criminal himself or to Civil Society, but must in all cases be imposed only because the individual on whom it is inflicted *has committed a Crime*. For one man ought never to be dealt with merely as a means subservient to the purpose of another, nor be mixed up with the subjects of Real Right [i.e. goods or property]. Against such treatment his Inborn Personality has a Right to protect him, even although he may be condemned to lose his Civil Personality. He must first be found guilty and punishable, before there can be any thought of drawing from his punishment any benefit for himself or his fellow citizens.

... If Justice and Righteousness perish, human life would no longer have any value in the world.—What, then, is to be said of such a proposal as to keep a Criminal alive who has been condemned to death, on his being given to understand that if he agreed to certain dangerous experiments being performed on him, he would be allowed to survive if he came happily through them? ... a Court of Justice would repudiate with scorn any proposal of this kind if made to it by the Medical Faculty: for Justice would cease to be Justice if it were bartered away for any consideration whatever.

Even if a Civil Society resolved to dissolve itself with the consent of all its members—as might be supposed in the case of a People inhabiting an island resolving to separate

8. Translated by W. Hastie (Edinburgh, 1887).

and scatter themselves through the whole world—the last
Murderer lying in the prison ought to be executed before the
resolution was carried out. This ought to be done in order
that every one may realise the desert of his deeds, and the
bloodguiltiness may not remain upon the people; for otherwise they might all be regarded as participators in the
murder as a public violation of justice.[9]

It is not that we are *justified* in punishing an offender, that we
have a moral right to do so but may, without moral failing,
choose not to exercise it. Rather we have a categorical obligation to impose a certain penalty: it would be wrong not to impose it. This is so, we are initially told, 'only because the
individual on whom it is inflicted *has committed a Crime*'. These
words, as well as other expressions of the supposed reason for
punishment, are open to several misinterpretations. They
might be taken to suggest, as on occasion they have been, that
we have a moral obligation to punish a man simply because his
act was against the criminal law as it stood. Such a claim, which
is quite unacceptable, is not to be confused with related ones.

(1) A judge may be *legally* obliged, or more likely permitted, to punish a man simply because his act was against the
criminal law. This is to say no more than that the law lays down
certain possibilities for the judge in such cases. For him to be
under a legal obligation, or for him to be legally enabled to
act, is for there to be a covering law. *We,* on the other hand,
are *legally* obliged not to interfere in the course of justice in
certain ways. None of these obligations and rights issues in the
conclusion that anyone is morally obliged or permitted to
punish. (2) A judge has a kind of moral obligation, one that
may be overridden by other obligations in certain circumstances,
to administer the law as it stands. He has undertaken to do this.
Similarly we may be under a kind of moral obligation, one
more easily overridden, to support the law as it stands. Breaking
even a bad law might have dangerous social consequences.

None of this, though, to come back to the original reading,
amounts to the proposition that we are under an absolute

9. *Op. cit.*, pp. 195–8.

moral obligation to punish a man simply because there was a law making an act he performed into a criminal offence.[10] It is notorious that there have been odious laws and completely unjustified punishments. That, however, is not the main point. When a man is punished under a law, however acceptable the law, a moral justification may depend on the morality of the law but not on the fact that there *is* a law. It will not depend on the fact that something has been specified by the correct authority as an offence. Kant's words, that we punish a man only because he 'has committed a Crime', require another interpretation if they are to be taken seriously. Such an interpretation is suggested in several places, notably by the assertion in the third passage that we are obliged to support a man's punishment *because it is his desert for his deeds*. In part the point is that he has acted wrongly or immorally, as distinct from only illegally. He has done something of a sufficient wrongfulness to be prohibited by law.

Notice, before we consider the meaning of desert claims more carefully, the nature of the supposed obligation. We are to observe (as we are elsewhere told explicitly) the *lex talionis:* 'an eye for an eye, a tooth for a tooth'. A man *must* be punished if he has performed an act for which he deserves a penalty. Further, he must not be given a lesser penalty than he deserves for his action even if it is true, as sometimes it is thought to be, that some lesser penalty will reform him or benefit others while the penalty he deserves will make recidivism likely. The obligation, however, is two-sided. A sane man who has obeyed the law must not be made to suffer even if this would have the good effect, for example, of keeping him from committing offences he otherwise is thought likely to commit. Further, given that every man must be treated exactly as he deserves, an offender's penalty must not be increased over what he

10. Something like this view was advanced by J. D. Mabbott, 'Punishment', *Mind*, 1939, and criticised by C. W. K. Mundle, 'Punishment and Desert', *Philosophical Quarterly*, 1954. A related doctrine, to the effect that to accept a law as both validly enacted and also immoral is self-contradictory, is espoused by Hans Kelsen, *General Theory of Law and State* (Cambridge, Mass. 1946), pp. 374–6, 407–10. Mabbott has subsequently put forward what I take to be a revised view.

deserves even if it is believed that a more severe penalty is needed as an example to deter others from the same offence.

It is worth reiterating, to avoid confusion and to distinguish this version of the retribution theory from others, that it is not a reminder that certain legal obligations exist, that there are laws which bind judges and also our own interventions in their procedures. Nor are we being reminded of moral reasons for support of the existing law, moral reasons of a relevant but not a conclusive kind. Nor are we being told that we are morally obliged to punish simply because there is a law against something. What *is* intended is partly that legislators, who regulate the practice of punishment partly by fixing scales of penalties, are obliged to arrange that men get what they deserve given the wrongfulness of their actions, *simply because they deserve it*. Legislators are not to take into consideration, in this respect, the well-being of offenders or of society as a whole. Judges are to proceed similarly in the fixing of particular penalties. We, finally, are obliged to support our legislators and judges.

To contemporary sensibilities and judgements this is harsh and unrealistic. Is there, perhaps, some misunderstanding? More than one philosopher has thought so. 'Does a person who advocates the retributive view necessarily advocate, as an *institution*, legal machinery whose essential purpose is to set up and preserve a correspondence between moral turpitude and suffering?' The answer given by the asker of the question is 'Surely not.' On the contrary, 'what retributionists have rightly insisted upon is that no man can be punished unless he is guilty, that is, unless he has broken the law'.[11] That is, perhaps, desert is a necessary condition of a justified punishment, but not in itself a sufficient condition. As we shall come to see, not everyone who holds what he calls a retribution view of punishment advocates a practice whose sole principle is to preserve some relation between immorality and suffering. It would be bizarre to suppose, though, that Kant's view in the quoted passages is no more than that a man may be punished only if a certain condition is satisfied. Certainly this prohibition on punishing individuals who do not deserve it is present.

11. John Rawls, 'Two Concepts of Rules', *Philosophical Review*, 1955, p. 7.

Equally certainly, there is the supposed obligation to punish those who are said to deserve it, and to punish them as much as they deserve. In other passages of the *Philosophy of Law*, inevitably, one hears other notes, but I shall not consider them. My concern is not really with exegesis but with the clarification and appraisal of one possible view about the justification of punishment. That it has been the view of many men is to me a certainty but not something for which I shall argue.

4. *Desert*

Let us now take one side of the supposed obligation, that we *must* punish to a certain degree in certain circumstances, and examine the reason given for it. The reason is that men deserve penalties. It has sometimes been given as a sufficient reason for the conclusion that we are justified or right in certain punishments, as distinct from being under an obligation to impose them. What will be said is as relevant to this argument. We must begin by getting clear what may be meant by the claim that a man deserves a penalty. It may be taken to mean a number of things, some of which have already been mentioned, and thus to be open to different objections and defences. To my knowledge no adequate differentiating analysis has ever been provided by either the defenders or the critics of retributivism.

(1) It is sometimes true that people say that a man deserves something and intend no more than that it is right that he get it. To attempt to argue that a man's punishment is justified, by saying in this sense that he deserves it, is obviously pointless. Any desert claim that reduces to the assertion that it is obligatory or permissible to impose a penalty cannot, of course, be offered as a reason for the proposition in dispute, that it is obligatory or permissible to impose the penalty. This is a simple fallacy where the supposed reason is identical with the supposed conclusion. It is a simple fallacy which may sometimes be concealed, as we shall see.

(2) What may also be intended by a remark that a man deserves a penalty is simply that he did act wrongfully. More precisely, he performed an action of a certain culpability.

This by itself has not been regarded by retributivists as a sufficient explanation of the supposed justification of particular punishments. I shall incorporate it after clarification into more adequate interpretations of desert claims, where it plays a part. Before doing so, we may discard some inadequate ones.

(3) What is usually meant or implied when it is said that a man deserves some particular penalty is that there is a relationship between it and something else. People may once have meant that imposing the penalty would involve an effect very like the effect of the man's offending action. A murderer might in this sense be said to deserve execution. What a man who commits rape or breach of promise deserves, in this sense, is a question which leaves room for reflection. A more important point is that any retribution theory that is worth discussion involves certain defences which may be offered by an accused man. They include the defences that he was grossly provoked and that his action was unintentional. Such defences are quite excluded by the claim that a man should be punished as he deserves, given the present notion of desert. It must be discarded.

(4) Someone may mean in saying that a man deserves a certain penalty for an offence that the penalty would bring about as much distress to him as he caused to someone else by his offence. This is in the neighbourhood of a more interesting contention. As it stands, however, it could not be part of any retributivism worth discussion. The reason is the same as before. Two men who by their offences cause the same distress, one intentionally and one accidentally, would be said in this sense to deserve the same penalty. No reflective retributivist has intended this notion of desert.

(5) To say that a man deserves a certain penalty may mean that he behaved culpably and that there is a relationship between his culpability and the distress of the proposed penalty. The relationship has been and still is commonly regarded as one of 'equivalence'. Whether it can sensibly be regarded in this way depends on the terms of the relationship. The culpability of an offender in his offence, we may briefly say, depends on two things: the harm caused by his action and the extent to which he can be regarded as having acted responsibly. Greater

culpability attaches to violent assault than to pilfering, given equally responsible agents. Greater culpability attaches to intentional as against accidental wounding. Given some such understanding of culpability, it is clear that no penalty can be regarded as either equivalent or not equivalent, in any factual sense, to a man's culpability in his offence. This is so because the distress of a penalty and the culpability of an offender are not commensurable.

(6) Reflection on forms of expression used by judges and others in place of 'because he deserves it' may bring to mind a different relationship. 'The punishment is right because he owes it.' 'He is to be punished because he must pay his debt to society.' I shall take it that what lies behind such claims, although disavowals may be expected, is that a man is rightly punished because his punishment brings satisfaction to others. In particular but certainly not exclusively it satisfies desires of the person or persons he has offended against. For a number of reasons of a cultural nature which we need not consider, this argument is rarely made explicit.[12] To ignore it is none the less to ignore what

12. I have, since writing this, come upon two passages that are relevant. Hermann Lotze, the nineteenth-century German philosopher, speaks of the vindictive satisfactions given to individuals, particularly the victims of offences, by punishment. He continues: 'Were these persons all so organised that they were incapable of feeling pleasure and pain, then it is self-evident that there would no longer exist . . . any right of punishment. . . . It is only the unhappy condition of feeling which takes place in the soul of the injured person that explains and forms the basis for new actions which aim to obviate the same.' *Outlines of Practical Philosophy*, translated by George T. Ladd (Boston, 1885), p. 98. James Fitzjames Stephen, the Victorian judge, writes: 'The punishment of common crimes, the gross forms of force and fraud, is no doubt ambiguous. It may be justified on the principles of self-protection, and apart from any question as to their moral character. It is not, however, difficult to show that these acts have in fact been forbidden and subjected to punishment not only because they are dangerous to society, and so ought to be prevented, but also for the sake of gratifying the feeling of hatred—call it revenge, resentment, or what you will—which the contemplation of such conduct excites in healthily constituted minds. If this can be shown, it will follow that criminal law is in the nature of a persecution of the grosser forms of vice, and an emphatic assertion of the principle that the feeling of hatred and the desire of vengeance above-mentioned are important elements of human nature which ought

has given force to retributivism. The relationship in question
may be described as holding between the grievance caused to
the victims of the offence and others, on the one hand, and the
satisfactions given them by the offender's penalty. 'Grievance'
may seem an odd choice of word here, but I think it the best
one. It would be mistaken, for example, to talk of the injury or
the deprivation caused to individuals as one term of the
relationship in question. This is so for the reason that we want
something which varies with the extent to which a man may
be regarded as responsible for his action. The grievances I have
in mind are those which a person may *have* rather than be *done*.
They are, we may say, desires for satisfaction, satisfaction which
comes via the experiences of certain individuals. Penalties may
be regarded as equivalent to grievances in the sense that they
precisely satisfy them. The distress caused to the man who is
penalised is neither less nor more than is required to satisfy
the grievance. It is important to see, however, that to defend
a man's punishment as deserved, in this sense, is not simply to
rest one's case on an equivalence. It is to defend the punishment as
giving satisfactions. That they *are* satisfactions is more important
than that they can be displayed as equivalent satisfactions.
Why should they be granted? If one forgoes suppositions about
tacit agreements by members of a society to keep the law, as
one must, the argument must be in the end that grievances
exist. They are desires, and like other desires they must be
taken into consideration.

To present desert claims so construed as an element of
retributivism is to run contrary to a prevailing orthodoxy. All
recent discussions of retributivism have regarded it as a
doctrine which finds a justification of punishing a man wholly
in his past action and a relationship between that and the
penalty *in so far as it affects him*. If, it is said, anything else is in
question, the doctrine is not retributivism or not only that. This
is to fall under the thrall of a definition and into misdescription.
It is to misdescribe the attitudes and arguments of retributivists.
They cannot much protest because they have not been self-

in such cases to be satisfied in a regular public and legal manner.'
Liberty, Equality, Fraternity (London, 1874), pp. 161–2.

aware or explicit. Their reticence, whatever is finally to be said of their argument, is misplaced: there is no reason for *ruling out of discussion* the claim that a course of action will lead to the satisfaction of desires. What is to be said for the orthodox view is that it pays a somewhat scholarly attention to the self-descriptions of retributivists. The consequence is that retributivism becomes mystery, a doctrine whose central proposition about equivalence, if not construed in such a way as to call out for dismissal, evokes mainly wonderment. It would be jejune to suppose, in this context, if not in others, that the persistence and force of the doctrine in question had no basis in intelligible argument.

(7) In saying that a particular man deserves a particular penalty people commonly allude to a certain system, a penalty system. Its nature can more easily be made clear by sketching a model of its construction. To begin in constructing such a system we reflect on actions of considerable harmfulness, including such as killing and the appropriation of property. The grievance to which they may be regarded as giving rise, however, is a function not only of their harmfulness but also of the extent to which the agents involved are responsible for their actions.

We initially fix a particular penalty for actions of a particular kind, say killing, given that they are actions for which the agents can be held wholly responsible. We then fix lesser penalties for actions of this kind where the agents are to a lesser extent responsible. In each case, the intention is to fix a penalty whose distress brings satisfactions to others roughly equivalent to the grievance they have been caused. What this means, of course, is that the penalty does satisfy, and does no more than satisfy, the grievance. What we have in the end is a set of rules which specify a particular penalty for each of a large number of actions. These are actions which cause grievance sufficient to call for satisfactions which can be had only by punishment. Other actions which cause grievance may be the objects of practices analagous to judicial punishment, where the penalties are less severe. It should be clear that the system need not involve supposed equivalences between penalties and the culpabilities of agents in their actions. A man's culpability or guiltiness may be judged, as we have seen, by the harmfulness of his action and the extent of his responsibility for it. These two considerations also determine what I have called the grievance he causes and it is this that is in question. It is this that may be regarded as equivalent to something else.

A number of objections may be raised against this account of the construction of a penalty system. Some of them are not relevant. No attempt has been made to do more than sketch a model. Many things are left out that would be essential to anything like a factual depiction of the actual development of penalty systems. Such a depiction is not the object of the enterprise. The object is only to bring into view certain possible principles.

It may be objected, more relevantly, that the construction assumes an assessment of grievances and satisfactions and there can be no 'objective' measure that can be used. What can be said in reply to this? The construction involves, centrally, the picturing of a situation involving (1) an offence, (2) the grievance to which it gives rise, and (3) the penalty that would satisfy it. The offence is identified by way of the harm caused and the degree of responsibility of the agent. To say as we ordinarily do that a man has been harmed in some way is to describe his state and also to do *something like* express an attitude of disapproval. 'Objectivity' objections, such as they are, are here in place. That a man's car has been taken away is as 'objective' a fact as that he is now on a bus. But has he been *harmed*? This is in part an evaluative question, and one that must be answered. Retributivists, in facing such questions, are no worse off than their critics and the holders of other theories.

If we are to identify offences, we must also take into account the responsibility of agents. Judgements about responsibility may also be described as factual. We recognise a considerable range of conditions which may reduce a man's responsibility for a particular action. He may be compelled to do something, perhaps in such a way that what he does barely counts as a case of action at all. He may do a thing without intending it, or fully intending it. He may act only after having been subjected to extreme provocation, or has a consequence of

illness or disability. There are many more such excusing conditions and we can order them as to their excusing capacity.
Needless to say, it will not be a simple list.

The point that emerges is that there is no insuperable
difficulty, of the sort envisaged by our objector, in the specification of an offence. It is not, in any fatal sense, a procedure of
'subjectivity'. If we turn now to the estimation, in general, of
the grievance caused by an identified offence, there again is no
such serious difficulty. That a man has a certain response to
the disappearance of his car is a consequence, in part, of
attitudes. What response he does have, what grievance he feels,
is a question of fact. It is a difficult question but not an evaluative one. It is partly to be answered, and this brings us to item
(3) above, by consideration of what satisfies him, what puts
an end to his grievance. Here again, in judging satisfactions, we
have what is fundamentally a question of fact, or at least can
be. So too, finally, is *our* question of equivalence: whether
penalties satisfy, fail to satisfy, or more than satisfy grievances.

We now have the claim that a punishment is justified, or
partly justified, by a man's deserving a particular penalty,
where this means that his penalty is in accordance with a
certain penalty system. Even given what has been said, this
remains in a way ambiguous. The argument cannot reasonably be, although sometimes this seems intended, merely that a
system of penalties exists, that it has been worked out or
enacted as law. It often seems, secondly, that in referring to a
penalty system a defender of punishment means to accept or to
underwrite it. He implies its moral acceptability. Given this, his
argument for punishment is similar to something mentioned
above, in connection with the very first understanding of
desert claims. It involves a form of the fallacy of *petitio principii*.
Very simply, he argues that punishment is justified in a particular case because it is justified in all cases of this kind. There is
another way in which the reference to a penalty system is of
significance. As I have implied already, to say a man's punishment is justified partly because it is in accordance with a
penalty system is to say that other men who have caused
similar grievances have been similarly treated and that the

same will be true of those who do so in the future. This is
something to be taken into consideration.

One final comment. Our actual practice of punishment is
undeniably governed by certain rules. These rules in some
manner or other connect particular offences with particular
penalties and may be classified in different ways. The description and justification of these rules, unlike their existence, is a
matter of question. A retributivist may regard them as the
outcomes of a construction of the sort just suggested. Their
purpose and justification, he will then say, is that they secure
that men get what they deserve. A very different account, as
we shall see, may be given by proponents of other theories of
punishment.

(8) There is also another acceptable understanding of
references to a penalty system, one of sufficient importance to
be listed separately. It may be implied of a man said to deserve
a penalty that he was aware of two options and free to choose
between them. He knew of the existence of a penalty system,
which is to say he knew of an intention and indeed an undertaking on the part of society to penalise certain actions. He was
aware, too, of the intention and undertaking *not* to penalise
other forms of behaviour. He knew of these options and chose
between them. He 'knew what he was getting into and needn't
have got into it'. He was responsible for his action.

(9) Suppose, finally, that two men have been given the
same opportunity to commit an offence, perhaps a theft in
conditions where discovery is highly unlikely. One succumbs
to the temptation and the other does not, and it is said that
one deserves a penalty and the other does not. What this may
be taken to mean, in part, is that it is in a certain sense fair
that one man and not the other be penalised. The offender has
presumably gained some satisfactions from his offence while
the other man has forgone satisfactions and perhaps even been
distressed by his renunciation. What we have, it may be argued,
is a situation where punishing the offender and not the other
man will be a move in the direction of equality of welfare and
distress. To say that one man deserves a penalty while the other
does not may be to convey, in part, just this.

5. *Defences and Criticisms*

Let us now put together the most defensible and complete interpretation of the claim, as ordinarily made, that a man deserves a particular penalty. It is (1) that he behaved culpably, (2) that the penalty will give satisfactions equivalent to the grievance caused by his action, (3) that similar ones have been and will be imposed on similar offenders, (4) that he was responsible for his action and performed it with a knowledge of possible consequences according to a penalty system, and (5) that unlike non-offenders he has gained satisfactions attendant on the commission of an offence. This might be complicated in various ways to avoid misunderstandings and objections but I shall not make it more cumbersome than it is. As it stands, it is worth consideration as a sufficient argument for punishing a man. It has never by itself been intended by anyone, partly for the reason that retributivists have commonly tried to defend their conclusions in ways we have already rejected. Untenable suppositions about factual equivalence between offence and penalty have been curiously persistent. If the argument as it stands is worth consideration, attempts might be made to strengthen it. Whatever use they have tried to make of notions of desert, retributivists have also appealed to certain general moral principles in support of their view. These have almost always been principles of justice, and they might be said to be relevant to our present version of retributivism.

There are many positive considerations in support of the retributive theory of punishment, if it is constructed as the theory that the vicious deserve to suffer. Firstly, it is a particular application of a general principle of justice, namely, that equals should be treated equally and unequals unequally. This is a principle which has won very general acceptance as a self-evident principle of justice. It is the principle from which the more celebrated, yet opposed accounts of justice, are derived. It is a principle which has wide application and which underlies our judgements of justice in the various areas. We think of it as applying—other things being equal—to fair prices, wages, and treatment

c

generally. It is in terms of such a principle that we think that political discrimination against women and peoples of special races is unjust, and that against children, just. Justice in these areas involves treating equals equally, unequals unequally—where the equals are equal in the relevant respect, and the unequals unequal in the relevant respect. Hence we think it just to deny women some jobs because of their weaker physique, but unjust to exclude a woman from a post such as a librarian or a violinist if she is more proficient as such than other candidates for the post. So too with justice and punishment. The criminal is one who has made himself unequal in the relevant sense. Hence he merits unequal treatment. In this case, unequal treatment amounts to deliberate infliction of evils—suffering or death.[13]

Notions of justice are difficult to handle with clarity, as this passage indicates. We might take it that the argument advanced is that there is a general moral principle that individuals who are equal in some respect are to be treated equally and in a way different from others. Does this provide support for the claim that those who can be said to deserve punishment, in our present sense, should be *treated differently* from those who cannot be said to deserve it? It may. Does it provide support for the claim that those who deserve punishment should be *punished* and those who do not deserve it should not? It does not. The principle would be satisfied, equally well, if we were to punish those who do not deserve it and not punish those who do. The principle would also be satisfied if we did no punishing at all and, say, repeated three times to ourselves the names of those who do not deserve punishment. *All* that the principle requires is that individuals who are equal in some respect should be treated equally and in a way different from others.

Let us try again. Perhaps the fundamental principle of justice in question is that individuals of the same desert are to be given their desert and that individuals of different desert are to be

13. H. J. McCloskey, 'A Non-Utilitarian Approach to Punishment', *Inquiry*, 1965, p. 260. The view advanced here is not wholly retributivist; this does not put in question the use I make of the passage.

given their different desert. The principle would be a general one, applying to all of life and not only that part to which punishment pertains. This is of relevance, at least, but the argument attached to it is hardly compelling. We are said to accept some such general moral principle and so to be committed to accepting a particular application or consequence of it, a particular justification of punishment. *One* reply is that we obviously are not governed in our actions and attitudes only by such a principle. We are also governed, if that is the word, by fundamental considerations of benevolence. We often think it right to forgo exaction of a man's deserts. There is thus no possibility of claiming that in consistency we must support punishment when it is deserved. What we must do, in this as in other problem-situations, is consider the force of arguments about desert among others. This will be our procedure.

There is yet another interpretation of the passage that we can try. It may be said that we share a principle to the effect that all people or all members of certain groups should be equal in satisfactions. If they become unequal in some respect, then some of them may be treated unequally in a certain way: a way that will restore equality of satisfactions. Those who commit offences gain in satisfactions. If we assume that a state of equality of satisfactions existed before the offences, what we must do is punish the offenders in order to restore the state of equality. Punishment will deprive the offenders of certain satisfactions and satisfy the grievance-desires of others. Again, it may be said of the general principle that it is certainly not the only principle relevant to our moral decisions. In certain cases, indeed, we do not follow it. Suppose a choice between (1) a policy which gives hardly any satisfaction, but an equal amount, to each of a number of people, and (2) a policy which gives a great deal of satisfaction to each of them but not an equal amount. The second is sometimes right.

However, it may be said that the principle is decisive with respect to the choice between punishing and not punishing a man. Here, *neither* course of action will improve the lot of everyone concerned. The punishment will take some satisfactions from the offender and give satisfactions to others. We do then have a general principle of justice, it may be argued, which gives us the conclusion that punishment is justified when deserved: when, in particular, it involves the exact satisfaction of grievances. *One* thing that may be said of this argument is that it depends upon a patently false premise. It is not true of our societies that their members are at any time equal or even roughly equal in satisfactions. As often as not the imposition of a penalty will make for less rather than more equality. Given our societies as they are, the general principle that individuals ought to be equal in satisfactions would direct us in at least a great many cases to the conclusion that we ought *not* to punish offenders.

Let us return to the fundamental retributivist argument for punishment, that men deserve it, taken by itself. What can be said against it? The enterprise of punishing men as they deserve involves assessments of their responsibility for their actions. It has often been objected[14] that such assessments are impossible or exceedingly difficult. The objection, already alluded to, can do with more attention. To assess adequately a man's responsibility, we are occasionally told,[15] we would require introspective knowledge of his state of mind at the time of his offence. We cannot enter into his consciousness. In the necessary absence of this, we have only his reports, and these are fallible and may be dishonest. A second objection is that we would require a full knowledge of his past development. We would require it to be able to determine to what degree it excuses him. In reply, it can be pointed out that it is easy to deny the possibility or practicablity of judgements of whatever kind by setting an impossibly high standard for acceptable ones. If what we must

14. See A. C. Ewing, *The Morality of Punishment* (London, 1929), p. 36 ff; W. D. Ross, *The Right and the Good* (Oxford, 1930), pp. 58–9; W. G. Maclagen, 'Punishment and Retribution', *Philosophy*, 1939; C. H. Whiteley, 'On Retribution', *Philosophy*, 1956; S. I. Benn and R. S. Peters, *op. cit.*, pp. 186–90. Brief attempts to defend retributivism are to be found in J. D. Mabbott, 'Punishment', *Mind*, 1939; C. W. K. Mundle, 'Punishment and Desert', *Philosophical Quarterly*, 1954; H. J. McCloskey, 'A Non-Utilitarian Approach to Punishment', *Inquiry*, 1965.

15. A. C. Ewing, *op. cit.*

have in order to assess a man's responsibility adequately is knowledge by introspection or by something like indubitable report, we can rarely if ever assess his responsibility adequately. But there is no reason for thinking that we need such knowledge. However, we do need a knowledge of his past. We must safely assume or know a good deal of his history in order to decide what he could, at any moment, have avoided doing. With respect to a number of the excusing conditions mentioned already, we must know of his past in order to decide if they obtain. The objection is that we require more than we can in practice have. In reply it must be admitted that there are effective limits to what can be learned by a judge of a man's past life. He may make use of inquiries but only to an extent fixed by a reasonable allocation of social resources. However, it may be said, it is at least possible to picture a workable procedure by which a judge or jury could be supplied with a sufficient knowledge of the histories of defendants. It is important to notice that retributivists are not committed to the defence of any actual judicial system in all its shortcomings.

It seems to be supposed, sometimes, that one can derive the same objection to retributivism by reflection on a particular difficulty.[16] There has long been a controversy over the definition of those offenders who are to be regarded as mentally ill or incapacitated and thus not responsible for their actions. The McNaghten rules in English law, recently modified, specified that a man was to be held responsible for an act unless he was labouring under such a defect of reason, from disease of the mind, as not to know the nature and quality of his act, or, as not to know that his act was wrong. The effect of this formula was to exclude from the class of the ill or incapacitated and thus not responsible any individuals incapable of acting on their knowledge. It excluded, in effect, many individuals usually regarded as ill or incapable and not responsible. Other difficulties, however, attach to other conceptions. I shall have more to say of relevance to this dispute in another place. What

16. See Barbara Wootton, *Crime and the Criminal Law* (London 1963). Cf. H. L. A. Hart, *Punishment and Responsibility* (Oxford, 1968), Chapter Eight.

is at present of importance is this question: Do difficulties of definition, in this borderline area, constitute a conclusive objection to retributivism? It seems that they do not. To grant that there are difficult or even undecidable cases goes no way to committing one to the conclusion that all or even many cases are undecidable or even particularly difficult. A retributivist impressed with the problems of judging responsibility where mental illness is a possibility might well dismiss the possibility of punishment. He could, in perfect consistency, maintain his doctrine with respect to the vast majority of offenders.

A second common argument against retributivism is that to say a man deserves a penalty is not to give anything that *could* count as a reason for punishment. That a man deserves a penalty is not a morally insufficient reason, but something that is not a reason at all, good or bad. A retributivist like Kant, we are told, refuses to consider such consequences or advantages of the practice of punishment as deterrence and reform.

It is therefore virtually impossible for him to answer the question, 'What justification could there be for rules requiring that those who break them should be made to suffer?' except perhaps in theological terms. For appeals to authority apart, we can justify rules and institutions only by showing that they yield advantages. Consequently, retributivist answers to the problem can be shown, on analysis, to be either mere affirmations of the desirability of punishment or utilitarian reasons in disguise. To the first class belong assertions of the type 'It is fitting (or justice requires) that the guilty should suffer.' For to say 'it is fitting' is only to say that it ought to be the case, and it is just this that is in question. To say, with Kant, that punishment is a good in itself, is to deny the necessity for justification; for to justify is to provide reasons in terms of something else accepted as valuable. But it is by no means evident that punishment needs no justification, the proof being that many people have felt the need to justify it.[17]

17. S. I. Benn and R. S. Peters, *Social Principles and the Democratic State* (London, 1959), pp. 175–6.

Consider three claims made here. The first is that an institution such as punishment can only be justified, if one forgets about appeals to authority, as we shall, by showing that it has advantageous consequences. The second, slightly wider, is that such an institution is only to be justified by giving reasons in terms of something else accepted as valuable. The third is that it is pointless to argue in such a way that one's argument reduces to the assertion that something is right because it is right. This third claim is a truism. What of the others? Is it true that an institution can be justified, appeals to authority aside, *only* by giving reasons for it in terms of something other than itself?

It is worth reiterating at this juncture that these are not intended as moral appraisals. It is not being maintained that no *morally adequate* justification of punishment can be given except in the way in question. Rather, what is advanced is a logical contention, one about what sorts of thing can count as justifications at all, adequate or inadequate. There are several logical points that might usefully be made about the notion of justification[18] but this is not one of them. To ask for a justification, in the way we are, is to ask for a sufficient reason for the acceptability or obligatoriness of something. Why should it be supposed that a description of whatever is being considered cannot count as a reason for its acceptability? Why should it be thought that a feature of something, or several features as in the case of punishment, cannot be the basis of its justification? It is a familiarity that various states of affairs, notably certain possible ends of human life, have been argued for in precisely this way. There is no reason for thinking that the same cannot be true of rules and institutions. Of course, to do so is now unfamiliar. Most people hold the moral view that the only adequate justification of a rule or an institution brings in its effects, but there is nothing to be gained by confusing this with a claim of another kind. It seems then that even if retributivism is so construed as to exclude all references to the effects of punishment, excepting those on offenders themselves, it cannot be put aside by a merely logical consideration.

18. See A. G. N. Flew, ' "The Justification of Punishment" ', *Philosophy*, 1954.

The argument, redescribed, is that one must regard retributi-vism as not offering a logically possible justification at all, or else as consisting in a certain disguised utilitarianism, a dis-guised attempt to justify punishment by its supposed deterrent or reformative effects. To take the second alternative would also be mistaken. It is not necessary to discount the often fervent denials by traditional retributivists that they take punishment to be of value for its supposed deterrent and reformative effects. If there are cases where it is necessary to discount such denials, these are quite atypical. This mistaken supposition that retributivism must often be taken in the suggested way, however, may derive in part from a truth. It is the truth already noticed that retributivism has been a forceful and widely held doctrine because it *does* imply that punishment gives a benefit. This is the benefit, as we have seen, of satisfactions produced by the imposition of penalties. We have construed the claim that men deserve penalties as implying, among other things, that the penalties will give satisfaction. We have thus construed retributivism as including this argument. To do so, obviously, is not to regard it as a theory of deterrence or reform under considerable disguise.

Consider now a more common-sensical argument against the belief that we are obliged or permitted to punish men in so far as they deserve it. Is it not *inconsistent* to condemn one man for injuring another and then to claim that society is morally correct to injure the offender in turn? Both the offender's act and the act of punishing him, it may be said, are contraventions of some principle, perhaps one of benevolence. The fact that the victim, in the case of punishment, has himself injured somebody else should not be regarded as making a sufficient difference between the two cases. If the first action was wrong, so is the second. Nor is there a sufficient difference to be found in the fact that in one case the injury is the work of a private individual and in the other the work of officers of a society acting in accordance with the law. Given this fact, punishment is not revenge. But if it can be defended only by considerations of desert then it, like revenge, is unjustified.

A retributivist can oppose this argument in a number of

ways. He may insist that there is a fundamental difference between a private action of one individual and the lawful actions of society. He need not but might introduce into the argument principles of democracy. He may say, further, that there is a fundamental difference between striking and striking back.[19] One may think a little or a lot of these considerations. What cannot be disputed is that the retributivist can rebut any charge of inconsistency. *His* principle of benevolence, he may say, includes a distinction between private actions and those of a society's authorities. Or, he includes in his principles, in addition to one having to do with benevolence, another having to do with desert. Injuries are wrong except in certain circumstances when they are deserved. Here there is no inconsistency. He might be asked by a critic, of course, to imagine a state of affairs where he himself was being punished. Would *that* be right? If the answer forthcoming is no, the retributivist may indeed have fallen into inconsistency. It is highly likely that he will accept that his own punishment, in the imagined case, would be justified. If so, his position is consistent.[20]

If these criticisms of retributivism are mistaken or insufficient, at least two others are not such. It is proposed to us that a man's punishment is justified or obligatory because (1) he has behaved culpably, (2) his penalty will give satisfactions equivalent to the grievance he has caused, (3) it will be similar to those imposed on other offenders who have caused similar grievances, (4) he was responsible for his action and knew of the possible consequences under a system of offences and penalties, and (5) unlike non-offenders he has gained satisfactions attendant on the commission of an offence. The first criticism is in a sense an external one. It has become increasingly apparent that there are many offenders who cannot be said to deserve penalties, in the sense just stipulated. The proportion of offenders who may be said to have been responsible for their actions is not so large as once was supposed. Over the past half-century

19. K. G. Armstrong, 'The Retributivist Hits Back', *Mind*, 1961.
20. An illuminating account of this sort of argument, involving among several things an appeal to someone to imagine himself in someone else's shoes, is given by Professor Richard Hare, *Freedom and Reason* (Oxford, 1963).

or so, it has come to be accepted that a considerable proportion of individuals who break the law cannot do otherwise. Given this, the retributivist must supplement his proposal for the control of criminality. Other practices than punishment are required. None the less, it may still be maintained, with respect to those offenders who can be said to deserve punishment, that their punishment is justified by the fact that they do deserve it.

One cannot reply that this contention, as we have understood it, runs against the conviction that there is no adequate reason for making men suffer, or for depriving them, if no good in human welfare comes of it. Retributivism does recommend a practice partly on the basis of accruing benefits. It would be difficult to explain its appeal, I have argued, if something like this was not true. One *can* reply, as I shall now explain, that retributivism runs against the conviction that benefits in the satisfaction of desires, to say nothing of other 'goods', must not be purchased at too great a cost.

To consider separately the elements of the retributivist argument, we are first given as a reason for punishment that some men have behaved culpably. I have included this supposed reason, here and before, out of a desire for completeness and with misgivings. It seems not to be a moral reason for action at all, good or bad. The fact, *taken entirely by itself*, that a man has caused a certain harm by a responsible action, seems to have no moral consequences. That is, as I shall come to explain more fully, it cannot be connected with any recognisably moral attitude. The second element of the retributivist argument, that punishment satisfies grievances, must neither be disregarded nor overestimated. The third is that a man's penalty will be similar to those imposed on offenders who have caused similar grievances. What needs to be said about this, for the present, is that it is in a way a secondary consideration. That is, a reason is advanced for choosing a particular system of punishment, one which is fair or consistent, if we are going to have some such system at all. Consider an analogy. If food is to be distributed to a group of people, some of whom are very hungry and some of whom are slightly hungry, we are likely to give a larger amount to each of those who are very hungry and a smaller amount to each of those who are slightly hungry. That we do anything at all, however, and that we feel that we ought to distribute any food, is not to be explained by that fact that all the members of one sub-group are in *one* state and all the members of the other in a different state. It is that they are all hungry. Suppose that there is a reason why all of the people in question should not eat for a given period. All of them are going to have surgical operations. We would not give them food, or feel we ought to, although some were very hungry and others slightly hungry. Similarly, the fact that some individuals have caused similar grievances, while others have caused dissimilar ones, is not in itself a reason for action.

The fourth element of the retributivist argument is that offenders have been responsible for actions which they knew to be offences and to carry with them certain possible consequences. This has usually been taken to be a reason for punishment although its nature has been left unclear. I shall for the present accept that it is a reason and postpone until later a fuller consideration which depends on acquaintance with doctrines so far undiscussed. Finally, we have it that offenders, unlike non-offenders, have gained satisfactions through their offences. Punishing offenders and not non-offenders, it may be said, contributes to the re-establishment of some earlier state of equality of satisfactions and distress. We have already noted, in our examination of the relevance to retributivism of general principles of justice, that this is entirely untenable in our societies as they are.

What emerges from this is that we must regard punishment as defended, finally, by the facts that it gives satisfactions to victims of offences and others and that offenders have freely and responsibly taken the option of committing offences. Obviously, if this is all that can be said for punishment, not enough can be said for it. We share a conviction that wants should be satisfied, and that they can justifiably be frustrated only under certain conditions. They may sometimes be frustrated if this course of action leads in the end to greater satisfactions. They may sometimes be frustrated in the interest of greater equality. Neither of these considerations applies in

the present case. It is not seriously arguable that the deprivations imposed by punishment on offenders and others is
outweighed by the grievance-satisfactions gained by victims
and others. Nor can it be argued that the course of punishment
can be defended by the principle of equality. It is not arguable
either that the deprivations of punishment are outweighed by
the satisfaction of grievance *and* the value, whatever it may
be, involved in the facts that offenders have freely and know-
ledgeably offended. This seems to me indubitable, but it
should not be taken for any other conclusion that it is. Quite
often it is supposed that *all* doctrines mentioning desert have
been exposed as masks for vengeance, that in our enlightenment
we need pay them no attention. An entirely general attitude,
one which takes all talk of desert to be pointless in all contexts,
cannot be sustained. This is a matter considered in the following
chapters. I should add that I will there give further accounts
of what is being appealed to when individuals are distinguished
according to whether or not they have acted culpably, freely
and with a knowledge of possible consequences, and so on. This
will not substantially affect the argument just given.

One final point to be made concerns strict and vicarious
liability. It will be apparent that the retributivist argument
which we have considered could not justify punishment where
a man neither intended to commit an offence nor was negligent.
Such a man could not count as deserving a penalty in the given
sense. Nor, of course, could the retributivist argument justify
punishing a man who merely occupied a certain position of
authority with respect to someone who performed a certain
action. This man, although 'vicariously liable' to conviction,
could not count either as deserving a penalty. Strict and vicarious liability, however, of which I shall have more to say, are
themselves matters of controversy.

6. *Annulment and Rights*

There is another retribution theory of very secondary
interest. We are obliged to punish, according to its first part,
since to do so 'is to annul the crime, which otherwise would

have been held valid, and to restore the right'.[21] A punishment is an annulment, a cancellation or a return to a previous state of affairs.

> If crime and its annulment . . . are treated as if they were unqualified evils, it must, of course, seem quite unreasonable to will an evil merely because 'another evil is there already'. To give punishment this superficial character of an evil is, amongst the various theories of punishment, the fundamental presupposition of those who regard it as a deterrent, a preventive, a threat, as reformative, etc., and what on these theories is supposed to result from punishment is characterised equally superficially as a good. But it is not merely a question of an evil, or of this, that or the other good; the precise point at issue is wrong and the righting of it. If you adopt that superficial attitude to punishment, you brush aside the objective treatment of the righting of wrong, which is the primary and fundamental attitude in considering crime. . . .[22]

Marriages, considered as contracts, can be annulled. Crimes cannot be, in any ordinary sense. My death or imprisonment, after I have killed a man, does not make things what they were before. In one way, none the less, my death or imprisonment does serve as an annulment. Hegel's argument begins from a conception of moral principles, such as the principle against taking another's life except, as we say, in certain circumstances. An act of murder is not merely a contravention of this principle but also a denial of its rightness. Such a denial is said to 'infringe' the principle. We must 'restore' it and this can be done only by punishing the offender. We are not to regard the crime as a harm done to someone, a mere 'evil', but rather as a denial of what is right. Nor do we 'restore' the principle because it is important for its effects in guiding conduct. We do what we do because the principle is right. To reproduce this doctrine more

21. G. F. Hegel, *Philosophy of Right*, translated by T. M. Knox (Oxford, 1942), p. 69.
22. *Op. cit.*, pp. 69–70.

faithfully and intelligibly would at least require a considerable and tedious excursus into the philosophy of Absolute Idealism. It has found a home elsewhere as well, in a tradition of English judicial thought. James Fitzjames Stephen, the Victorian judge and law historian, finds a justification of punishment in its 'ratification' of a morality which has been violated.[23] Lord Denning has observed that 'the ultimate justification of any punishment is not that it is a deterrent but that it is the emphatic denunciation by the community of a crime'.[24]

It is Hegel's suggestion that offenders not only break moral principles but deny their rightness. They speak, perhaps, a language of action. How is the principle infringed? Are we to understand that it becomes more open to question by individuals? The argument would then be that simply because a principle is differently regarded we are justified in punishing. This argument is *not* that this new attitude to the principle may issue in certain effects, notably the commission of offences. It would then be tantamount to a version of the arguments from deterrence and reform.[25] We are to punish, given our present supposition, simply because of a change of attitude. This, of course, is nonsense. However, it is quite clear that the supposed infringement of a principle has to do with more than individual attitudes. Hegel's intention, as distinct from those of some of his followers, is to be understood only by way of reflection on his view of moral principles, which are embodiments of Spirit. Not a great deal of advantage can be had at this point by consulting the related views of the English Idealists. Bosanquet, for example, speaks of crime as having a bad effect on 'the

23. As Professor Hart has pointed out in *Law, Liberty and Morality* (London, 1963), p. 63.

24. *Report of the Royal Commission on Capital Punishment*, s. 53.

25. In the passage just quoted it seems plain enough that Hegel finds no justification of punishment in its practical effects. However, interpretation involves difficult appraisals of his many reflections. In one of the additions made to the text of the *The Philosophy of Right*, on the basis of lecture notes, he is represented as saying that in some states of society 'an example must be made by inflicting punishments since punishment is itself an example over against the example of crime' (p. 274). Deterrence seems in the air.

general mind', which is not to be confused with even the collection of individual minds, mere 'atomic states of conscious-ness'.[26]

Let us recall that we have taken the position that individuals should not be deprived or made to suffer, no matter what they have done, if insufficient good in the form of human welfare or equality comes of their experience. We now have the claim that punishment has the consequence of restoring a moral principle which has a kind of independent reality. We are not to count in any possible effects on human conduct of this restoration. We might in reply question the truth or more likely the meaning of the metaphysical doctrines in question. The result might be that punishment does not have the restorative consequences attributed to it, for there are no consequences of that kind. A simpler and more economical course is to assume what can be assumed of the suggested view of moral principles. The question then arises as to whether the restoration of a moral principle so conceived is something sufficient to justify the practice of punishment. I take the answer, given our commitment to the avoidance of unnecessary suffering, to be no.

A second part of Hegel's account of punishment concerns the 'rights' of offenders to be punished. One line of argument proceeds from the assumption that men are in some part of themselves rational. Thus, they all recognise the obligation to punish offenders, presumably the obligation based on the need to restore a principle. They recognise this obligation even if they are offenders. They have a right, furthermore, to be enabled to fulfil this obligation. One's response to this, of course, is that a right that cannot be escaped is an odd right. Essays in the psycho-analysis of argument are not often profitable but it is hard to resist the feeling that the claiming of rights to punishment on behalf of offenders is most interesting as a projection of feelings of guilt or conscience. Let us admit, for purposes of economy of thought, that offenders have such a right *if* there exists the supposed obligation. The obligation, however, has not been established. This part of the doctrine too, incidentally, is not

26. Bernard Bosanquet, *Some Suggestions in Ethics* (London, 1918), pp. 190–6.

without its more recent adherents. 'If we respect personality,' we are told, 'we must respect responsibility. If we respect responsibility, we must respect the right of offenders to be punished for their offences.'[27] A second line of argument about rights, sometimes confused with the first one, is mentioned by Hegel in the following passage.

> The injury [the penalty] which falls on the criminal is not merely implicitly just—as just, it is *eo ipso* his implicit will, . . . his right; on the contrary it is also a right established within the criminal himself, i.e. in his objectively embodied will, in his action. The reason for this is that his action is the action of a rational being and this implies that it is something universal and that by doing it the criminal has laid down a law which he had explicitly recognised in his action and under which in consequence he should be brought as under his right.[28]

Implicitly, in his rational self, the offender accepts that punishment is obligatory and demands the right to fulfil this obligation. By his act, however, we are now told, he explicitly establishes a certain principle: that it is right to injure others. In consistency, again since he is rational, he accepts that this principle should be observed even when it leads to himself being injured—by punishment. Again, he claims a right. We need not exercise ourselves over whether an offender can be supposed to assert a principle such that his offence is a consequence of it. Nor need we wonder about what sense can be attached to the resultant demand that he be treated according to the principle. Let us suppose he makes the demand, or can be said to have a right. The question then arises of whether or not we ought to meet the demand or act on the right. That we ought to has not been shown.

It is worth noting, finally, that one Hegelian scholar[29] has

27. Ernest Barker, *Principles of Social and Political Theory* (Oxford, 1951), p. 179.
28. *Philosophy of Right*, p. 70.
29. J. M. E. McTaggart, *Studies in Hegelian Cosmology* (Cambridge, 1901), p. 137.

presented a different interpretation of the arguments about rights, an interpretation which might indeed be extended to cover the previous argument about annulment. It is that an offender may be *reformed* by punishment, and that he claims this reformation as his right. It is not that punishment, perhaps imprisonment, provides authorities with an opportunity to reform a man by one means or another. It is that punishment itself, the experience of suffering or deprivation, has a reforming effect. This interpretation of Hegel has often been accepted. Certainly it requires a curious reading of the first passage quoted above as well as others. It produces a supposed justification of punishment of a kind to be considered below.

D

2
Deterrence

1. *Factual Presupposition*

RETRIBUTIVISM is often characterised as an account of the justification of punishment which looks to the past. It is contrasted in this with the deterrence theory, and also reform theories, which are truly said to look to the future. Retributivism as we have conceived it, however, is not an argument that a man's punishment is justified wholly by an event in the past, his offence, or a relation between that and his penalty. It includes the contention that a man's punishment provides satisfactions. It must be taken to include this if we are to have a realistic characterisation of one persistent attitude, or a related set of attitudes, to offenders and their punishment. Given this, retributivism is to an extent similar to the deterrence theory. It does rest, albeit in a different way and to a lesser extent, on supposed consequences of punishment. The two differ in this: the deterrence theory finds no justification for action in a past offence, which has no more than a certain evidential importance, and it depends upon consequences of punishment other than the immediate satisfactions given to victims of offences and others. It need not ignore these satisfactions.[1] It rightly finds them of relatively small importance. What is taken to be of supreme importance is that punishment prevents offences.

General prevention ought to be the chief end of punishment as it is its real justification. If we could consider an offence which has been committed as an isolated fact, the like of

1. See Bentham, 'Principles of Penal Law', p. 383, in *The Works of Jeremy Bentham*, Volume One, edited by John Bowring.

which would never recur, punishment would be useless. It would be only adding one evil to another. But when we consider that an unpunished crime leaves the path of crime open, not only to the same delinquent but also to all those who may have the same motives and opportunities for entering upon it, we perceive that punishment inflicted on the individual becomes a source of security to all. That punishment which considered in itself appeared base and repugnant to all generous sentiments is elevated to the first rank of benefits when it is regarded not as an act of wrath or vengeance against a guilty or unfortunate individual who has given way to mischievous inclinations, but as an indispensable sacrifice to the common safety.[2]

Bentham goes on to suggest that punishment may prevent the occurrence of offences in three ways: by making it impossible or difficult for an offender to break the law again, at least in certain ways; by deterring both offenders and others; by providing an opportunity for the reforming of offenders. Some but not all punishments prevent offences in the first way, by incapacitation. Imprisonment tends to rule out the possibility of more offences by the offender for a time, except those he can commit in prison. The death penalty does, and fines generally do not, incapacitate. With respect to the second way of prevention, if we describe it in the usual insufficient way, punishing a man may make him less likely to offend again because of fear or increased prudence and may act in the same ways to deter others. As for the third way of prevention, punishment may be a means to changing a man's character or personality so that out of *some* motivation like consideration for others he obeys the law. In this chapter we shall be concerned with only the first and second reasons for punishment, incapacitation and deterrence, considered as sufficient by themselves. It will not be seriously misleading, I hope, to refer to them together as the deterrence theory.

It is a supposition or at least not an established truth that punishment does in fact deter people. Are many deterred? If so, are they deterred from *all* offences or is some other explanation

2. *Op. cit.*, p. 396.

to be given of why they do not commit some offences? Philosophers have very rarely if ever considered such questions. Most often this has been a consequence of an assumption that punishment does deter to some significant extent. Recently it has been a consequence of a general reluctance to engage in factual controversy, controversy which can be settled (if at all) only by other than philosophical methods. I share this reluctance, overborne as it has been by a reluctance to leave wholly unconsidered an essential part of both the argument in hand and arguments to come. I shall say relatively little.[3]

What is in question? It is suggested that because of the possibility of punishment some significant number of potential offenders, individuals contemplating possible offences in a serious way, do not in fact go ahead. Other men who find themselves in situations which they did not anticipate or intend, perhaps situations where they are provoked, are said to be restrained by the prospect of a penalty. Others who do commit certain offences are restrained from more serious ones because of the greater possible penalties. They sometimes take self-preserving steps, such as not carrying weapons. The individuals in each of these three classes may not have been punished in the past. The explanation of their behaviour may be fear of punishment, some other aversion to it, or a prudential calculation. What is typically not mentioned is the further proposition that the practice of punishment may have a role in the creation, transmission, and reinforcement of the unreflective attitudes of many people for whom the question of breaking the law never or rarely arises in a serious way. Certainly *any* single-factor explanation of this common behaviour would be mistaken. At the same time, it would be rash indeed to ignore the factor of punishment.

There are some statistics of a certain relevance.[4] It is very

3. A more extended discussion may be found, for example, in Nigel Walker, *Crime and Punishment in Britain* (Edinburgh, 1965), Chapter Twelve.

4. Criminal Statistics for 1966 (Home Office, London). Difficulties in the use of criminal statistics, which I do not consider, are excellently surveyed in Barbara Wootton, *Social Science and Social Pathology* (London, 1959), Chapter One.

evidently the case that much more crime is committed by the young. Among men and boys in England and Wales in 1966 the age-group with the largest number of convictions for indictable offences was that of the fourteen- to sixteen-year-olds. There were 3,199 offenders per 100,000 of the population. (Among boys under fourteen, the rate was 1,622 per 100,000.) In the the age group of those seventeen or over and under twenty-one, the rate was 2,944. In the group of those twenty-one or over and under thirty, the rate was 1,867. For those thirty and over, the rate was a mere 385 per 100,000. The conclusion is inescapable that a very large number of offenders do not come back to the attention of the courts after the age of thirty or less. The conclusion that these statistics do anything like 'prove' the factual assumption of the deterrence theory, of course, *is* escapable.

The figures have to do with men and boys who have been found guilty, which is not to say punished. Large numbers of convicted offenders, particularly in the lower age ranges, are discharged or placed on probation. What we can safely say, then, is that very large numbers of individuals do not come back to the attention of the courts after either having been punished or having been made particularly aware of the prospect.

The figures are for those found guilty, not for all men and boys who commit indictable offences. It might be said that the figures are consistent with the supposition that many offenders, as they grow older, continue to break the law but avoid apprehension or conviction. Perhaps a sufficient reply to this is that while older individuals may be more capable of avoiding apprehension and conviction, those who are younger are often not charged but dealt with in other ways.

The figures do not establish what proportion of offenders become law-abiding as they grow older *because of* the experiences of punishment or having been made particularly aware of the possibility. The figures are consistent with the supposition that a large proportion of young offenders become law-abiding adults because of something having nothing to do with punishment. Perhaps there is a process of maturation which leads to law-abiding behaviour and would do so as effectively without punishment or a heightened awareness of it. One of the things we need, and have not got, is statistics on boys who break the law but are never apprehended or convicted. What is their later behaviour? If we stick with the statistics we have, our response to them must depend on the conviction that is carried by alternative explanations of them. The explanations open to the deterrence theorist, the propositions mentioned above, are certainly not obvious losers. The boys in question, he may say, are by their experiences made more fearful of or averse to punishment, or simply more prudent. One very common reply is that such explanations, or some of them, involve a fallacious assumption, 'that we are rational beings, who make a careful calculation of possible gains and losses before deciding upon our actions'. It is fallaciously assumed, 'in the Benthamite phrase, . . . that we always act in accordance with our own "enlightened self-interest"'.[5] On the contrary, the explanations of why individuals break the law are of a very different nature. Some commit offences for the excitement, and it is hardly a surprising fact given the quality of their lives. Others, the victims of guilt-feelings unrelated to crime, are not deterred by the prospect of punishment but positively attracted to it. Still others, in varying ways 'abnormal', are equally far from any prudential consideration of possible consequences of their actions. Only one-third of discovered murderers are sentenced as 'mentally normal', it may be said, and of these a large number act in conditions or situations where 'rationality' is anything but likely. Finally, it may be added, it is a truism that people do not choose between possible courses of action in a prudential way if the possible consequences of one course are distant in time and the consequences of the other immediate. A penalty is a distant possibility; the gain from an offence is usually immediate.

This is confusion if intended, as it sometimes seems to be, as *a general reply* to the explanations of the deterrence theorist. He may admit without reluctance that many of those who commit offences are for one reason or another not influenced by the possibility of punishment. It certainly does not follow,

5. Howard Jones, *Crime and the Penal System* (London, 1956), p. 140.

however, that those who *do* obey the law are not deterred. It can hardly be claimed that the possibility of punishment must be as uninfluential in the conduct of the majority who obey the law as it is, in different ways and degrees, in the conduct of the minority who do not. The fact that 'non-rational' grounds of behaviour are decisive with some individuals is not good evidence that they are equally decisive with all or many others. Moreover, it is clearly a mistake to suppose that the claim of deterrence must simply be that individuals 'calculate' and compare the possible gains of offences and the possible losses through punishment, that they judge what is in their best interests and act on their judgements. That punishment leads to law abidance through 'non-rational' processes is quite as important as part of the deterrence claim.

If the institution of punishment plays no part in securing that young offenders become law-abiding, what alternative explanation can be given? There is no explanatory value in passing references to the possibility of 'spontaneous recovery'. To say that there occurs a 'process of maturation' is similarly unhelpful.[6] Doubtless, something which can be so called does occur, but would it have the supposed consequence, obedience to law, in the absence of an institution of punishment? In the absence of an adequate alternative explanation, it is difficult to resist the belief that young offenders are affected by their experience. It is also difficult to resist the belief that individuals who never offend are influenced in a related way. Such conclusions, however, require qualification. They are, as they stand, much too general.

As I have implied, the argument would be improved if a correlation could be shown between youthful law-breaking, *without* apprehension, and subsequent offences. One should not expect, given the deterrence supposition, a *strikingly* high connection. The supposition is in part that the practice of punishment has a deterring effect on individuals other than those convicted of offences. It is reasonable to suppose that this effect is also a function of such things as expectations, obligations, and settled wants that increase in strength and number

6. See Wootton, *op. cit.*, Chapter Five.

during early life. None the less, one would expect some correlation of the kind mentioned. Statistics are unavailable here because those who conduct research cannot get hold of the relevant control group: young unapprehended law-breakers. There is a bit of evidence of a related kind, however, related in that the situation in question involved a belief, in this case well founded, that the possibility of punishment was remote. It supports the belief in deterrence and also is one of several considerations that suggest that a considerable modification of that belief is necessary.

A unique opportunity for making an evaluation of the deterrent approach to crime was presented by Danish experience during the war. In 1944, the German occupying forces deported the Danish police, and for some time the country had only a local guard force invested with police authority. There followed an immense rise in the number of robberies, thefts, frauds, etc., but no comparable increase in murder or sexual crimes. While this experience does show that crime is reduced very considerably by the prospect of detection and presumably punishment, it suggests that deterrent methods are of less value in reducing the incidence of those crimes in which strong passions or deep psychological problems are involved.[7]

One might raise questions about this case, which is one of behaviour in an abnormal situation, the occupation of a country in wartime. One might also resist any implication that it is only rarely that robberies, thefts, frauds, and other 'ordinary' offences are the product of 'strong passions or deep psychological problems'. None the less, there is some support to be had here for the contention that the prospect of punishment has a considerable deterrent effect with respect to many offences. That it does not have this effect with respect to *other* offences is a probability as well supported by general psychological theory. In this connection one might also remark that punishment's *having* a deterrent effect with respect to many offences is at the

7. Jones, *op. cit.*, pp. 141–2.

very least consistent with a good deal of psychological theory. The practice of punishment, one may say, gives support to the super-ego.[8]

I shall have more to say of relevance to the claim that punishment does deter many potential offenders. Many reformative theories of punishment rest a good deal on a denial of it. My present inclination, in which I shall persist, is that there are adequate grounds for supposing that the practice of punishment does greatly reduce the incidence of a large group of offences. To take the view that it does not have a comparable effect with respect to another considerable group of offences, however, is to accept that the application of the traditional deterrence theory is much more limited than has been supposed. That theory, as I shall explain more fully in a moment, has always been that punishment is justified only under certain conditions, one of which is that it must deter to a certain extent. It is a traditionally recognised consequence that some offenders should not be punished. What is now evident, however, is that Bentham and other supporters of the theory considerably underestimated the numbers of offenders whose punishment is unlikely to have an acceptable deterrent effect.

A first conclusion of our discussion, then, one that will be given more support when we come to reformative accounts of punishment, is that the contemporary deterrence theorist is left with a significantly large class of offenders whose punishment is of doubtful value. He must then add something to his recommendations and in effect depart from a programme for dealing with offences based only on deterrence. It does remain a possibility, despite what has been said, that the punishment of many offenders is morally justified on grounds of deterrence alone. For all that has been said, punishment as a part of a larger programme may be acceptable simply because it deters.

2. *Economical Deterrence*

That it is not so justified is the conclusion of a number of

8. See for example J. C. Flugel, *Man, Morals and Society* (London, 1955), p. 208.

moral rather than factual arguments, most of them to the effect that punishment governed only by the intention to deter is inhumane or unjust. Despite its notoriety, it is said, retributivism is more humane. Some of these criticisms derive from taking into consideration a parody of the deterrence theory. They suppose that what is being claimed is that *any* punishment is justified if it serves to keep the offender and possibly others from committing offences in the future. It is said that this is the deterrence principle *per se*, and that if we acted on it we would be perfectly justified in attaching savage penalties to certain minor offences if such penalties were required in order to deter potential offenders.[9] It has been remarked, for example, that the principle would justify flogging a man for a parking offence, since flogging would certainly have the effect of deterring him and others from parking their cars in the wrong places.[10] It is quite true that such repugnant consequences follow from the simple principle that any punishment is justified if it deters. For that reason such a principle is far from morally acceptable. No one would regard it as a defensible principle, and it would be absurd to suppose that Bentham, for example, puts it forward. Whether or not it can be correctly described as the deterrence principle *per se* is unimportant.

Bentham's view, partly, is that a penalty may be justified only when the distress it causes to the offender and others is not greater than the distress that would result if he and others, undeterred, offended in the future. Punishment is an 'evil' because it causes pain both to those who suffer it and others, and also because it limits the freedom of those who obey the law because of it. Offences, obviously, are an evil to the victims. Both evils, that of the punishment and that of the kind of offence in question, must always be considered. 'If the evil of the punishment exceed the evil of the offence, the punishment will be unprofitable: the legislator will have produced more suffering than he has prevented; he will have purchased exemption from one evil at the expense of another.'[11] We then

9. A. C. Ewing, *The Morality of Punishment* (London, 1929), p. 52.
10. K. G. Armstrong, 'The Retributivist Hits Back', *Mind*, 1961.
11. Bentham, *op. cit.*, p. 397.

have it that punishing a man is justified if it deters and if the suffering, misery, or anxiety involved is not greater than that which would result if he were not punished. One further addition is desirable. It may be true that any of a number of possible punishments would deter and in so doing cause less distress than would otherwise occur. If this is the case, of course, only that particular punishment is justified which causes the least distress. We then have the principle that a man's punishment is morally justified if the following conditions are satisfied. It does indeed deter and in so doing (1) causes less distress than would occur if it were not imposed. Also, (2) there is no other punishment that would deter as effectively at a cost of less distress. Punishments which satisfy these conditions have been called *economical deterrents* or punishments that deter economically. The usage, of course, does not have to do with the economics, in the sense of financial cost and profit, of punishments. I shall use the term 'economical deterrent', and speak of punishments deterring economically. References simply to deterrent punishments and to deterrence are also to be understood as references to economical deterrence. It may be in point to reiterate, in anticipation of later arguments, that punishments may fail to satisfy the given pair of conditions in several ways. If they may cause too much distress to the offender, they may also cause too much to persons other than the offender who are affected by the fact of his punishment. The connection may be very indirect, and by way of other offences. It is also to be noticed that the conditions have other consequences as well. Penalties must be sufficiently severe to deter effectively. It has sometimes been true that offenders regarded the penalties for their offences as like licences: an unavoidable feature of conduct of a certain kind and not so undesirable as to be a deterrent. Such penalties, on the view we are considering, have no justification.

Of the pertinent criticisms of the deterrence view, a vague one advanced by Kant is that to punish a man simply because this will deter him and others from offences in the future is to treat him only as a means and not as an end. This might be taken to refer to several supposed moral errors and it is important to distinguish them. (1) To treat all men as ends and not merely as a means may be to take into account, in any particular situation, the personal welfare of each and every individual involved. We should, that is, consider the interests of each individual affected by a different possible course of action before coming to any decision. Under this interpretation of the rule that all men are to be treated as ends, it is at least arguable that the deterrence theory observes it. According to the theory, certainly, the degree of suffering caused to the offender is relevant to the question of whether or not his punishment is justified. (2) What may be intended, however, by a critic who employs Kant's rule, is that the deterrence theory does not give sufficient attention to the interests of the offender. Such a claim has sometimes been advanced by some of those who argue for a justification of punishment in terms of a supposed reformative function. They suppose that punishment protects the interests of others by reducing the number of offences, and serves the interests of the offender by reforming him. Punishment is not justified simply by the prevention of offences. We are not yet in a position to assess the claim about means and ends when so interpreted. It amounts to a version of the reform theory. (3) Sometimes the rule about treating men as ends is at least partly intended to convey the injunction that men are to be treated as responsible moral agents, which they are supposed to be. What is recommended here is a general attitude, difficult to encapsulate, which takes as supremely important the supposed fact that men make free decisions for which they are accountable and which place limits on our treatment of them. This attitude issues naturally in support for the retribution theory of punishment and in particular criticisms of the deterrence theory. These and other criticisms I shall now consider in more detail. There is nothing to be gained by retaining Kant's terminology.

The criticisms attempt to display the deterrence theory, even in its reasonable form, as having entirely unacceptable consequences. Unusual and well-worn cases are produced where punishments that may seem unjustified, given our ordinary moral convictions, appear to be justified by the principle of economical deterrence. We are asked to suppose, often, that on a particular occasion a judge knows that the man before him is innocent of the offence with which he has been charged. He knows too that there is no possibility of apprehending the actual offender. Finally, he knows that the offence that has been committed will be followed by others of the same kind unless the potential offenders are deterred—unless, that is, someone thought to be guilty is punished for the offence that has been committed. Given all this, we are invited to conclude that the judge would be justified by the stated principle in *pretending* that the man before him was the actual offender and imposing a penalty on him. Why not punish him? This would, we suppose, have the effect of preventing other offences, which would involve more distress than that caused to the innocent man by his punishment. This effect would follow from the belief on the part of others that justice had been done; that the man was not really guilty would be irrelevant to this fact.[12] In short, if one maintains that punishment is justified by deterrence alone one seems committed to the immorality of punishing the innocent. It seems that one is committed to denying the rule that only the guilty may be punished. Surely, then, the deterrence theory is unacceptable.

The traditional rejoinder to this traditional criticism is that imposing a penalty on an innocent man, first appearances to the contrary, would *not* result in economical deterrence. Let us first consider some recent attempts summarily to dismiss the criticism. The first amounts to the reminder that the deterrence principle of punishment is about punishment and that it attempts to justify this and nothing else.[13] That is, the principle is about an authority's infliction of distress *on an offender*. The

12. 'In point of utility apparent justice is everything, real justice, abstractedly from apparent justice, is a useless abstraction, not worth pursuing and, supposing it contrary to apparent justice, such as ought not to be pursued.' Bentham, *Principles of Judicial Procedure*, *Works*, Volume Two, p. 21.

13. Anthony Quinton, 'On Punishment', *Analysis*, 1954. For a view similar in some respects see John Rawls, 'Two Concepts of Rules', *Philosophical Review*, 1955. See also S. I. Benn, 'An Approach to the Problems of Punishment', *Philosophy*, 1958, and Benn and R. S. Peters, *Social Principles and the Democratic State* (London, 1959), pp. 182–3.

principle, it is said, simply does not apply to the case imagined, where a man known to be wholly innocent is made to suffer. Since the man is not thought to be an offender by the judge it is quite mistaken to suppose that this is a case of punishment. In calling it such, we have been forgetful of the description of punishment given above in the first chapter, one of a kind stipulated by defenders of the deterrence theory. We might better say, although the term may have some misleading connotations, that the imagined case is one of *victimisation*. The deterrence principle has nothing to say about victimisation. It is not the principle that imposing a penalty on *anyone*, if it deters economically, is justified. It is that punishment, the imposing of a penalty on a man who is an offender, is justified if it deters. This forceful reply has been thought inadequate by a number of philosophers, although they have not done much to despatch it. We are told, for example, that the given reply prevents us from considering the question of whether the deterrence theory does justify the imprisonment of innocent men. So it does, and for a given reason which must be considered. It is true that the deterrence principle as stated does not appear to commit one to sending innocent men to prison when this would serve the end of deterrence. This seems odd. One expects that it is at least a possibility, if no more, that the deterrence theory has such a consequence. Can it be that the contrary seems true only because the view has been stipulated in a particular way? That this is so can be shown.

According to the theory, punishment is justified by the fact that it deters *and for no other reason*. The anticipated result, a state of affairs involving fewer offences, secured at a certain cost of distress, is by itself a sufficient justification. It is not the case that the means to this end, punishment by itself, has any separate and additional justification. The contrary is explicitly said to be true by utilitarian defenders of the theory, for the simple reason that punishment consists in the causing of distress to offenders. Punishment is valuable only as a means to a desirable end. If one keeps these facts in mind, it becomes apparent that the following formulation, 'Punishment is justified when it deters economically', is misleading as a formulation of the deterrence theory. By referring only to punishment, which necessarily is of offenders, it implies a falsehood. That falsehood is that the deterrence theory taken by itself has some feature such that its holders could not possibly be committed to acts of victimisation. There is no such feature. All that is relevantly impossible is that they are committed to acts or practices that do not serve as economical deterrents. The theory can be formulated in a way that overtly excludes this false implication. For all that has been said so far, there can be no objection to expressing it in the following more general way: 'A society's practices or actions in dealing with criminal behaviour are justified if they deter economically.' So expressed, it is at least a possibility that acceptance of the view commits one to victimisation in certain circumstances. If it can be established that certain victimisations would deter, and if we accept that such victimisations are not morally justified, the conclusion follows that the view which sanctions them is unacceptable.

This argument may give rise to an uneasiness, one which can be dispelled. It may be thought that there is an arbitrariness about the reformulation of the deterrence theory. Might it not be defensible for a proponent of the theory simply to persist in his own, that *punishment* is justified only by the consideration that it deters economically? This and only this, he says, is what he means. He may do this, but without gain. His intention is to give a justification of punishment but evidently he is bringing to light only part of what he counts as its justification. It is impossible to avoid the conclusion that he regards punishments as justified not only because they deter but because those who suffer them have committed offences. If this were not the case, then certain victimisations too would be acceptable to him. It must be that he refuses to defend them because they lack a feature had by punishments. He has implicitly abandoned a straightforward deterrence account for something else. He can *either* take up what I have called a compromise view of the justification of punishment, one which includes some require-ment of guilt, and so avoid accepting the possibility of certain justified victimisations, *or* he can take up the deterrence view and accept the possibility of such consequences. Our present concern is with the latter view.

There is also another attempt that might be made to deal summarily with the speculations about victimisation to which the critic of the deterrence theory has recourse. One cannot but feel a certain suspicion about the producing of cases where it is claimed that judges, according to the theory, would be committed to secret acts of victimisation. The suspicion, misidentified, may issue in the comment that if we are to keep in touch with social realities, something better must be found by way of criticism. What might better be offered, it may be suggested, are descriptions of social practices that might actually be established in the usual way. Might we have 'an institution . . . which is such that the officials set up by it have authority to arrange a trial for the condemnation of an innocent man whenever they are of the opinion that doing so would be in the best interests of society'?[14] The officials might be judges of the higher courts together with police authorities, the minister of justice, and members of the legislature. But when one considers the possibility of such an institution, which would be established by law and a matter of public knowledge, one sees that it would involve very great dangers. One need only mention the possibility of abuse of power and the creation of a general insecurity among members of the society. It cannot seriously be supposed that someone who defends punishment by the argument that it is an economical deterrent would be committed to the institution we have imagined. It is entirely too likely that the losses would exceed the gains.

Such a reply must begin from a misconstruction of the traditional objection to the deterrence theory. That objection does not involve, nor need it, the specification of some social institution different from punishment. There is no reason why the objection should proceed by specifying some possible publicly known practice and by arguing that such a practice would have a justification given the deterrence theory. There

14. Rawls, *op. cit.*, p. 11. The argument I am considering is combined with several others in this paper. I treat of them separately.

is no reason why the objection should not isolate some possible action and relate it to the deterrence theory. The logic of the argument does not require even that the action in question be one by an officer or officers of a society. We are told that the one and only, and a sufficient, justification of punishment is that it deters economically. There are *no* other justifying features. If so, *any* action or practice which does deter economically must be morally acceptable. If it is not, then a question arises about the claim that punishment is justified *solely* in virtue of being deterrent. The simplicity of the objection reflects the simplicity of the claim. What I am maintaining, then, is that in criticising the deterrence theory one is in a way free to choose one's counter-examples. One need not initially meet *any* demand but that they be examples involving victimisations which might be of an economical kind. *Reductio ad absurdum* arguments are not essays in social theory. Certainly this is but the first step of the argument. One must go on to establish that in the cases in question it *would* be true that victimisation would prevent more distress than would otherwise occur. The traditional position of those who hold the deterrence theory, to which we now turn, is that this cannot be shown. The suspicion one does feel about the cases in question is that in the end the suggested victimisations would not be economical. This suspicion, we are told, is not merely reasonable but well founded.

3. *The Consequences of Victimisation*

We have on the one hand defenders of the theory, who have maintained that it does not in fact ever issue in victimisation. They agree, secondly, that victimisation would never be morally acceptable. We have on the other hand the critics, who maintain that the theory does or would in certain circumstances justify victimisation. They declare, secondly, that victimisation is not and would not ever be morally acceptable. Their reason for the latter belief is that victimising a man is *treating him in a way that he does not deserve*. As we shall see, both defenders and critics are in error, defenders with respect to both of their

E

propositions, critics in supposing that it is absolutely impossible
that a victimisation should be morally justified.

Our practice of punishment is taken to be governed by
certain rules, such as the rule that the guilty but not the
innocent are to be penalised. Other rules are to the effect that
offenders of greater culpability are to receive greater penalties.
Grievous assault carries a heavier penalty than petty theft,
injury that is fully intentional a heavier penalty than inadver-
tent injury. For the retributivist, as we have seen, the point of
these rules is that they secure that men are treated as they deserve.
The rules are taken to comprise a penalty system of the kind
whose construction was sketched in the first chapter. To the
traditional deterrence theorist their point is quite otherwise.

They are rules whose observance secures that we deter
economically. To depart from them, in one direction, is to
engage in what we have been calling victimisation. Victimisation, according to the argument, is never justified by the
deterrence theory because it is never economically deterrent.
Let us look at the details. With respect to the rule about punishing only the guilty, one insufficient claim has its origin in
the truth that if we are to prevent offences by punishment we
must direct our efforts toward the right individuals, those
likely to offend in the future. One kind of evidence that a man
is likely to break the law in the future is that he has done so
already. To act on this evidence in picking out potential
offenders is to obey the rule about punishing only the guilty.
It may also be added that it is by punishing those who have
already performed certain actions that we affirm or reaffirm to
others what actions are offences and thus to be avoided. These
considerations may serve to give an explanation of why in
many cases we should abide by the rule in question. But let us
return to the first case of possible victimisation mentioned
above. Here, a judge reasonably believes that secretly victimising an innocent man is necessary if other individuals are to be
deterred. We assume he has good grounds for thinking they
will commit the offence in question unless they are deterred.
Admittedly, there may be no evidence that the defendant
needs deterring, but that cannot settle the question. A standard

rejoinder is that such an act of victimisation is unlikely to have good results on the whole, despite the possibility or even the certainty that sentencing the man might in the short term deter a number of potential offenders. Sentencing the man would be to take an exceedingly dangerous step, one whose distant consequences are all too unpredictable. It *might* happen that one victimisation would lead to others, and it might become *known* that innocent men were being penalised for offences committed by men never apprehended. It might then be supposed that actual offenders escaped punishment with considerable regularity. One upshot would be that potential offenders of all kinds would cease to be deterred to the same extent as before by the possibility of punishment. A man is the less deterred the less certain it seems that he will be punished for an offence.

Another result, one of several, might be that the law would be brought into disrespect. This claim, never long forgotten in this context by defenders of deterrence, is in part that people respect the law because they believe it deals fairly with individuals. This respect would be lessened by a belief in the existence of victimisations. Who can say what the consequences of such a lesser respect for the law might be? All these are no more than speculations, certainly. But who, we are asked, could be reasonably certain that developments of this sort would *not* follow from the judge's action in breaking the rule that only the guilty are to be punished? If one could not be reasonably certain, one could not accept that such an action would in the end make for economical deterrence. This is little more than a sketch for an argument, obviously; the processes by which victimisation might issue in the supposed consequences would be complex.

Penalising the innocent is but one possible kind of victimisation. Other kinds involve infractions of the other rules of punishment. These can be divided, artificially, into two groups and we shall concentrate on the second. There are those which provide heavier penalties for offences involving greater harms, for example, grievous assault against petty theft. Here, the deterrence theorist explains, economy is obviously the justification. The other rules, which may be roughly described as having to do with the responsibility of agents, have been divided into three kinds.[15] There are those, first, which allow that in certain circumstances a man is *justified* in a kind of action which in other circumstances would be criminal, and so is not to be punished at all. Killing in self-defence is sometimes an example. Secondly, there are rules which specify that a man is to be *excused* in certain circumstances and not punished at all. He may be excused if his action was in some way quite involuntary or unintentional. Finally, there are rules specifying that a man's punishment is to be mitigated under certain circumstances. If he can establish, for example, that he was subjected to extreme provocation, he may receive a lesser penalty. In choosing the particular penalty from the range fixed by statute for offences of the kind in question, a judge is to take into account provocation.

The explanation and justification of these three kinds of rules, according to the deterrence theorist, is also that observing them serves the end of economical deterrence. Their explanation and justification has nothing to do with desert. A man who injures another in self-defence on one occasion gives no evidence that he is likely to injure others again unless he must do so to defend himself. He is no more a danger to the community than most other men. If it does happen that he is attacked again, then he will be justified in defending himself: we do not take the view that he should be deterred from doing so. The same is true of anyone else who is attacked. Thus there would be no point whatever, on the deterrence view, in punishing the man on this occasion. In general, to follow rules of justification is to act in accordance with the principle of deterrence. Somewhat similar considerations apply to actions covered by rules of excuse. A man who injures another by an entirely unlikely accident gives no indication of being a generally dangerous character. Nor would punishment on this occasion prevent either him or others, obviously, from causing accidental injuries in the future. There is no point in punishment, given the

15. H. L. A. Hart, 'Prolegomenon to the Principles of Punishment', *Proceedings of the Aristotelian Society*, 1959–60. See also Richard Brandt, *Ethical Theory* (Englewood Cliffs, N.J., 1959), Chapter Nineteen.

deterrence view, where rules of excuse apply. As for the rule of extenuation having to do with provocation, a man who retaliates only under extreme provocation is unlikely to offend again, since extreme provocations are few. There is some possibility, nevertheless, that he will be provoked in the same way again. What is required to make it likely that he will resist this future provocation, if it occurs, is no more than a lighter penalty on the present occasion. We suppose, that is, that a man who has resisted a good deal of provocation before succumbing on the first occasion will need only a slight additional motive derived from a relatively mild punishment in order to resist a bit more in the future. Thus there is no need for a heavier penalty on the first occasion: it would be wrong to impose it since it would cause more distress than is necessary. One can present much the same argument, such as it is, with respect to other potential offenders, who must also be considered. One supposes that they are unlikely to be subjected to such a provocation. In general, the danger is small. If they are so provoked, one supposes that they will be deterred from giving in if they have been influenced by no more than the example of a relatively mild punishment. If we are to deter economically, then, we must not victimise by breaking rules of extenuation.

Such considerations go some way to showing that abiding by rules of the three kinds is in accord with the deterrence theory. Nevertheless, they have a general and considerable weakness.[16] Consider the argument that observing a rule about provocation is a necessity if we are to deter economically. It hangs together, or appears to, only because certain of the future possibilities and not others are considered. This can be brought out by way of a model. Brown injures a man who has provoked him by harming his dog. Brown's penalty is reduced, according to the deterrence argument, partly because there is little danger of his offending again. People are unlikely, we suppose, to be after his dog very often, or to be doing things that are similarly provocative. We suppose, furthermore, that Brown will not need very much by way of a new motive to keep him from repeating his offence *if the same sort of occasion arises again.*

16. See also Hart, *op. cit.*

Looking to other possible offenders, they are unlikely to be provoked to the same extent in the future, since such provocations are relatively rare. If they are so provoked, they will not succumb to the provocation if they know Brown has been lightly penalised—*if, that is, they are as self-controlled as Brown.* But what if we look to other possibilities in the future? What if Brown's dog is harmed *and,* true to form, his flowers are trampled? Perhaps he would resist the temptation to retaliate by inflicting a serious injury if in the past he had been given a heavier rather than a lighter penalty for injuring someone who kicked his dog. What of other potential offenders who are not as self-controlled as Brown? Suppose one of them was to see his dog being harmed or was provoked to about the same extent. Perhaps he would retaliate even if he knew Brown had been given a relatively light penalty but would not do so if he knew Brown had been given a heavier one. When we consider such possibilities, and there is no reason for ignoring them, it is not at all clear that sticking to the rule of mitigation in question is called for by considerations of economical deterrence. Indeed, it seems that the principle in question might demand infractions of the rule. It is equally arguable that if deterrence is our only guide we might be committed to breaking rules of excuse, to punishing a man who injured another by accident. Our severity might well have the effect of preventing possible offences in the future. It might serve to prevent intentional offences and to make avoidable accidents more rare. Something of the same sort may be argued in connection with some offences covered by rules of justification.

Are there effective rejoinders to argument of this kind? In the case of the first rule-infraction, that of penalising a wholly innocent man, it was open to the defenders of the deterrence view to argue that such a victimisation might in the long run issue in more rather than fewer offences. Our present cases are different. We suppose, for example, that a judge believes on good grounds that potential offenders will be deterred only if he makes a striking example of a man, which involves breaking the rule about mitigation. Here it is not so open to holders of the deterrence view to suggest that the outcome, in the long term, may be more rather than fewer offences. We cannot readily suppose that if the judge's action becomes known, potential offenders will be the less deterred. On the contrary, they may be more deterred by the fact of the judge's rule-infraction. However, we may still worry about the possibility of disrespect for the law. There is also another argument.

Rules of excuse and mitigation, aside from those of them having to do with certain special classes of offenders such as children, have the effect of excusing, wholly or partly, actions that are less than wholly voluntary or deliberate. This means that to a considerable extent the possibility of a man's being penalised, or heavily penalised, depends on his deliberate and voluntary actions, those over which he has control. He thus can be reasonably confident, if he wishes to be, that his life will not be disrupted by judges. Precisely this security would be endangered if the rules of excuse and mitigation were sometimes suspended. The danger, although distant, would exist. It *could* come about that a man could no longer be reasonably confident of an undisrupted existence if his intention was to obey the law. Accidents happen. It can thus be argued that while breaking the rules of excuse and mitigation might sometimes have a greater deterrent effect than keeping them, the cost in anxiety or something like it that might result from breaking them would outweigh the profit. Such an argument is open to anyone who takes up the position that punishment is justified when it deters economically, although it has sometimes been suggested otherwise. It has been supposed, perhaps, that anyone who makes use of it must be appealing to retributivist considerations. It has been supposed that the argument is rooted in a principle of justice or fair play. Quite obviously, an argument *could* be presented which would begin from the premiss that each man should get what he deserves and proceed to the conclusion that the rules ought to be observed. This is quite distinct from what has been presented.[17]

17. Hart, *op. cit.*, argues that it is impossible to explain the rules of excuse and mitigation by reference to deterrence and then goes on to explain them by the consideration, for example, that they increase 'the power of individuals to identify beforehand periods when the law's punishments will not interfere with them. . . .'

It has sometimes rightly been admitted by defenders of the deterrence theory, for all that has been said, that in a *conceivable* case of a very special nature a judge would be committed by the deterrence principle to an act of victimisation, even the penalising of a wholly innocent man. It has been admitted, that is, that one can imagine a case involving such certain secrecy, etc., as to rule out the possibility of long-term dangers. However, it is said, it is entirely unlikely that there will ever be an *actual* case which satisfies the imagined conditions. This fact has sometimes been thought to vitiate the argument.

> . . . if one considers . . . fantastic situations . . . one does of course consider them as a person with certain moral sentiments, the strength of which, in society as it is, is an important Utilitarian good. These sentiments are offended. A Utilitarian will see no point in trying to imagine oneself looking with approval on the imaginary situation, since this is likely to weaken the feelings while not serving as a preparation for any actual situation. If in fact punishing the innocent (say) always is and always will be harmful, it is likewise harmful to dwell on fanciful situations in which it would be beneficial, thus weakening one's aversion to such courses. Thus the Utilitarian shares (quite consistently so) in the unease produced by these examples. Although he may admit that in such a situation punishment of the innocent would be right, he still regards favourably the distaste which is aroused at the idea of its being called right.
> Certainly if one imagines the world as other than it is, one may find oneself imagining a world in which Utilitarianism implies moral judgements which shock our moral sentiments. But if these moral sentiments are quite appropriate to the only world there is, the real world, the Utilitarian is glad that moral judgements in opposition to them seem repugnant. He sees no need for moral acrobatics relevant only to situations which in fact are quite out of the question.[18]

Our present objection to the deterrence theory involves three

18. T. L. S. Sprigge, 'A Utilitarian Reply to Dr. McCloskey', *Inquiry*, 1965, p. 274.

considerations which I shall state in order to comment on this
rejoinder. They are:

(1) the proposition that in a certain conceivable case victim-
    isation would deter economically,
(2) the consequence that such a victimisation would be called
    for and justified by the principle of economical deterrence,
(3) the acceptance that such a victimisation would not be
    morally acceptable.

How does the argument in the quoted passage function? Does
it attempt to call into question (1), (2), or (3)? One might think,
confusedly, that (1) is the object of the argument. But it is not
being maintained that in such a case victimisation would not
deter economically. It is simply being claimed that to *accept now*
that such a victimisation would deter economically may have
bad effects. Given a commitment to the deterrence theory, one
would have to accept that the imagined victimisation would be
right. Accepting this, it is supposed, might weaken one's
general aversion to victimisation, which aversion is perfectly in
place with respect to actual cases. The speculation may be that
one might be led not to disapprove of victimisations in actual
cases, where they are not economical. We can accept all this
without comment. It leaves undisturbed the hypothesis that
in a conceivable case the action of victimising a man would
deter economically. We can suppose, if with reservations, that
a Utilitarian judge who contemplates our conceivable case
comes thereby to approve of or to bring about victimisations
that do not deter economically. This does not matter; we can still
conceive of the case we want. Can it then be that the argument
is intended to falsify (2), that the principle of economical
deterrence would justify the conceivable victimisation? The
argument cannot possibly succeed in showing this to be false.
There is a logical connection between the principle, the
specification of the case, and a conclusion that victimisation
would here be justified. Finally, can it be supposed that the
argument is aimed at (3), that the imagined victimisation would
be wrong? Clearly enough, it is accepted that the victimisation
in question would be without moral justification.

There is one further possibility. It might be thought that while the argument does not disturb any of (1), (2), or (3), there is implicit in it another forceful criticism. Is the objection to the deterrence theory in a way toothless? All that it establishes, it might be said, is that in a case which is unlikely ever to obtain the principle of deterrence would give us a consequence we regard as unacceptable. This, it may be said, should not trouble us. The principle remains acceptable, for all that has been said, for the real world, and that is what we are concerned with. The reply is that we are indeed concerned with the real world and in particular with our practice of punishment. The objection against the deterrence theory, involving a merely conceivable case, appears to tell us something about a possible justification of that practice. It is that the practice cannot be justified by considerations of economical deterrence alone. We have been offered the principle that our practice has no justification whatever other than that it deters potential offenders at a certain cost of distress. This by itself, none the less, is said to be sufficient. *If* this were true, then a certain conceivable case of victimisation would be justified. If we do not accept this, and *do* accept that punishment may be justified, then it must have more to recommend it than merely that it deters economically. It should be clear that the fact that this argument rests on a conceivable rather than a likely or an actual case is of no importance. What is important is the specification of the case and the moral view that is taken of it.

4. *Necessary Distinctions*

We have now surveyed, in something like its own terms, a persistent dispute. Sadly enough, it ignores certain very relevant facts. As has been pointed out,[19] we already *have* within the law what are regarded by many as justified victimisations. We *have* departures from rules of excuse and mitigation. Precisely what is true of a defendant charged under a strict-liability statute is that he is *not* excused because he did not intend to commit an offence and was not careless. The shopkeeper who sells adulter-

19. First, to philosophers, by Hart, *op. cit.*

ated milk, in complete ignorance of the fact and despite having taken reasonable care to avoid doing so, cannot offer this as a defence. The rationale that is offered, of course, is that the dangers of adulteration are so considerable that they must be avoided even at the cost of certain victimisations. Some of those who regard rules of excuse as essentially rules for securing that men get their deserts and only their deserts would claim that the dangers are so considerable that they must be avoided at the cost of treating some men in a way that they do not deserve. Convictions where defendants are vicariously liable are defended in the same and other ways.

Quite as important, we are familiar with victimisations where strict and vicarious liability is not in question. They are, indeed, absolutely common. Defendants who have been found guilty of certain offences are given penalties which judges announce to be 'exemplary' ones, penalties calculated to satisfy what is taken to be a considerable need for deterrence. In England cases involving train robbers and espionage agents provide outstanding examples. More everyday examples result from the theft of coins from telephone kiosks and acts of physical assault. It would be a work of benighted piety to argue that the penalties which are imposed are in general precisely those called for by the rules of justice ordinarily thought to govern our practice of punishment.

I wish, at the moment, to say two things about these facts. The first is that it is arguable that we do here have *actual* victimisations which deter economically. The last persuasive objection to their being such cases, it may be recalled, was that victimisations would give rise to a general insecurity and anxiety which would make them, in the end, uneconomical. This has not been the effect of the creation of offences of strict and vicarious liability. Nor has it been an effect of exemplary penalties. The second thing to be said, although I wish to put off a final consideration of strict and vicarious liability, and also exemplary penalties, is that it is arguable that these victimisations have a moral justification. With respect to exemplary penalties, it is at least sometimes true that they are not much greater than the penalties that would be imposed given a strict adherence to the rules. Also, the need for deterrence may be regarded as substantial. Many of the penalties imposed under statutes of strict and vicarious liability are relatively small ones, or relatively easily borne by the defendants. As I have said, the dangers to be avoided may be regarded as great.

Given these circumstances, obviously, the argument about the deterrence theory must take a different form. The defenders of the theory need not labour to maintain that any conceivable victimisation would be uneconomical. If certain victimisations would be economical, but also have a moral justification, they constitute no objection to the deterrence theory. Critics of the theory, on the other hand, must do more than show that certain victimisations would be economical. They must establish (as we so far have not) that these would not have a moral justification. Is it possible to produce such cases?

We can proceed to an answer by seeing more clearly what it is that makes certain victimisations at least possibly justified. With respect to at least some strict liability offences, it can be said that there exists a great danger to *each* of a considerable number of individuals. Offences of selling decayed foods are an example. Also, the penalty imposed on the shopkeeper is certainly such as to cause him less distress than would be caused to each of a number of individuals if they were poisoned. When a man is given an exemplary penalty, once again, it can be argued that there exists a great danger to each of a considerable number of individuals. Also, it may be argued, the additional distress caused to the offender, over and above what he may be said to deserve, is usually relatively small. There is also something else to be kept in mind. It is not essential that for a possibly justified victimisation the penalty in question must be a relatively small one. Utilitarians in their zeal to avoid the traditional objection to the deterrence theory have often not seen one clear possibility of defence. In that objection, as we have seen, it is vaguely said that in a certain case a judge would be justified in the secret victimisation of an innocent man. Instead of hurrying to reply that this would be uneconomical in the long run, one might reasonably demand a further specification of the case. Is it a completely extraordinary one where the judge may literally be said to *know* that a considerable number of offences will be committed unless there is a deterring example? Is it certain too that nothing else would work? The answers must be in the affirmative, it may be said, if the argument is to be coercive. Let us also suppose that the penalty imposed on the innocent man would cause him extreme distress, and something like the same distress as would be caused to each of the victims if the potential offenders were not deterred. If *this* is what we are to consider, we have a situation in which there exists a choice between very considerable distress for one innocent individual or roughly the same distress for each of a considerable number of innocent individuals. The commendable response of most people, given such a situation, is to look for some other option. *If* there is no other option, however, it seems undeniable that the victimisation of the defendant would be morally preferable. We have not got an economical victimisation that is morally indefensible.

What brings us, however unwillingly, to admit the possibility of justification in all these cases is that (a) there is a considerable danger to each of a group of individuals to be avoided, and (b) the distress that would be caused to the victimised individual is relatively small or no greater than that which would be caused, given no victimisation, to each of the group of individuals. Obviously we *can* conceive of a case without these saving features. It will be one where there is a great danger to be avoided, and which can be avoided *only* by a victimisation involving very great distress to the individual in question. Most important, it will be one where the distress that would occur, without the victimisation, would be *widely spread*. That is, the danger in question is that *each* of *very many* people would suffer relatively little. In total, which is all that is important given the deterrence view, the distress would be such as to make the victimisation, despite its severity, economical. Here it is not an arguable proposition that the victimisation would be morally tolerable. We do not think that an extreme imposition of distress on one individual is tolerable if the alternative distress for others, however great in total, is for any particular individual bearable. We are governed in this, clearly enough, by a principle of equality. Given that distress is inevitable, and that all the individuals in question are equally vulnerable or undeserving, we choose that distribution which most closely approximates to an equal one. In our present case, that distribution is the one which involves no distress for the single individual in question, the defendant, and not a great deal for anyone else. What remains is to see what final conclusion can be drawn from this sequence of argument.

We do have a case of economical victimisation, it seems, which would not be regarded as morally justified. It must then be that punishment if justified has some recommendation other than that it deters economically. That recommendation, obviously, is that it excludes the possibility of a kind of grossly unequal treatment. We may conclude that any acceptable justification of punishment must rest in part on its being *deserved*, in a somewhat unusual but not unreasonable use of the term where it means no more than that the practice does exclude grossly unequal treatment. Objectors to the deterrence theory might at this point wish to argue for a more general conclusion: that punishment is partly justified because it is deserved in the sense defined above in the first chapter. There we supposed that to say a man deserves a penalty is to say (1) he has behaved culpably, (2) his penalty will give satisfactions equivalent to the grievance he has caused, (3) it will be similar to those imposed on other offenders who have caused similar grievances, (4) he was responsible for his action and knew of the possible consequences under a system of offences and penalties, and (5) unlike non-offenders he has gained satisfactions attendant on the commission of an offence.

5. *Comparisons*

One might try to argue, in the interest of establishing the more general conclusion, that we are *also* opposed to the victimisation because the victim did not deserve a penalty, in the sense of the words defined by way of the five propositions just mentioned. That the victim would not deserve the penalty in this sense, it might be said, contributes to our opposition.

That offenders do in this way deserve penalties, it might be said, contributes to the justification of punishment. I should like to consider this question along with another one. In order to gain a certain expositional advantage, let us turn to a different if related situation. We have until now followed a traditional line by considering cases of victimisation where it is supposed that there is no possibility of securing a similar deterrent effect by punishment. Why not consider situations in which there is a choice between punishment and victimisation? It seems indubitable that if we have a choice between a punishment and a victimisation, where each is thought likely to deter to the same extent, we would prefer the punishment. Why is this true? Is it to be explained, more adequately than in the traditional utilitarian arguments, by the fact that the punishment would be more economical? Is it to be explained by the claim that the punishment would be, in our full sense, deserved? *To what extent is this latter claim distinct from the claim that punishment would be more economical?* In order to answer these questions I should like to attempt the further analysis of arguments about desert which was promised in the first chapter.

It is worth while and perhaps essential to imagine a case in which one's responses would be the stronger and clearer for reasons of personal involvement.[20] The dangers are obvious enough to be avoidable. If a friend were the victim I would in opposing his victimisation certainly assert that it was undeserved. I would mean in part, according to our understanding, that he had not acted culpably. He did not cause a harm by an action for which he could be held responsible. Would this constitute a moral objection? On what feelings would this part of my claim rest? It would rest, it seems, on feelings which derive from something like instinctual responses both to injury inflicted on oneself and injury inflicted on others.[21] It seems undeniable that we share such responses. Furthermore, when there is no question of someone's having inflicted an injury, of being an assailant, it is not that we have *no* related feelings about he himself being injured. It is rather that we feel an

20. Cf. R. M. Hare, *Freedom and Reason*, especially Chapter Six.
21. Cf. Mill, *Utilitarianism*, Chapter Five.

opposition to his being injured, one which derives from the desire to retaliate against actual assailants. A good deal might be said of a psychological nature in explanation of these facts. More relevant is the question of whether these feelings can be regarded as giving rise to a moral claim. It seems to me that they cannot. It approaches certainty that the retaliatory response to assailants cannot be regarded as generative of a moral argument. My inclination is to take a similar view of those *related* attitudes to individuals *which depend entirely on their not being assailants*.

Could I reasonably intend, secondly, in saying that the victimisation would not be deserved, that it would not give satisfactions equivalent to *the grievance caused by the victim*? Assuming that the victim did not commit an offence at all, there is no such grievance. None the less, a grievance exists, that one caused by whoever did commit the offence in question. *This* grievance might indeed be satisfied by the victimisation, if the individuals who feel it take the victim to have been the offender. It seems, then, that in opposing the suggested victimisation I cannot say that it is undeserved where this means it would not provide certain satisfactions.

Consider now the third contention that might be contained in the judgement that the victim would not deserve the penalty: if he were imprisoned he would be being treated in a way different from the way in which other non-offenders are treated. Why do I resist this? Let us suppose, in order to have one irrelevancy firmly out of the way, that neither in this victimisation nor in the possible punishment would the distress caused to the victim or offender be considerably greater than that which would be caused to each of the victims of future offences in the absence of a deterring effect. My resistance, then, is not based on a conviction that distress, when necessary, ought to be distributed equally or as near as can be. I suggest that it is based on the following facts. As a consequence of the general truth that apprehended offenders are treated as they are, and non-offenders left to go about their lives, members of each class have certain expectations or regard certain things as possibilities. The non-offender in question, in being treated as offenders are treated, would be subjected to a special distress: shock, frustration, continuing apprehension. He would, as a consequence of his expectations as a non-offender, be subjected to a particular distress that would not be experienced by the offender if he were punished. Certain other things being equal, he would experience a greater distress. What we can conclude, I suggest, is that in opposing the victimisation on the ground that it would not be deserved, I would in part be opposing it as uneconomical when compared with the punishment. In part, I suggest, arguments from desert dissolve into arguments to the effect that deterrent punishments should cause as little distress as possible.

Fourthly, I should have in mind in opposing the victimisation that the victim was not responsible for the commission of an offence, that he did not act in contravention of the known system of offences and penalties. What would make this a reason against the victimisation? Again, it seems to me that it is a reason simply in virtue of the existence of certain expectations. The victim acted in accordance with the law and as a result had certain normal anticipations. To treat him as if he had broken the law would give rise to special distress. Before saying more of this explanation, which is likely to give rise to resistance, I should like to complete the inquiry in which we are engaged. In opposing the victimisation as undeserved, I could be taken to be maintaining, lastly, that the victim did not gain satisfactions attendant on the commission of an offence. That is, he did not disrupt any state of equality of satisfactions by committing an offence. The difficulty about this argument, as may be anticipated on the basis of what has already been said, has to do with the assumption of states of equality. It is perfectly possible that if we took into account the actual lives of members of the given society, the victimisation *would* have an equalising effect.

I take it that opposition to what has been argued will mainly have to do with the claim about the absence of a responsible action in contravention of the penalty system. Can it be maintained that in opposing the victimisation on the ground that the victim did not perform such an action one can only be

F

arguing that the punishment would cause less distress? Consider another choice with which we might be faced. It is again between a victimisation and a punishment but here it is strictly true that each would cause the same distress to the individual involved. The victim, we suppose, would undergo a distress consequent on his having had certain expectations. However, because the offender is somehow more vulnerable, offender and victim would experience about the same distress. We shall also assume, of course, that the distress caused to others in the two cases, perhaps family dependants, would be roughly the same, and that punishment and victimisation can be taken as equally effective with the respect to the prevention of offences in the future. It remains true, I think, that one's immediate response is that the punishment would be preferable. It is also unquestionable that many people would defend this preference by saying that the offender deserves and the victim does not deserve a penalty. One can readily imagine someone going on to explain: 'The victim simply did not do what the offender did. There is an immense difference between his past conduct, which was lawful as a consequence of a decision or resolve of his, and the conduct of the offender, who did make a choice or decision to break the law. Either of them could have broken the law and one did not. The point in this imagined case is that the offender has freely contributed to the situation in which he finds himself and the victim hasn't.'

This crucial case leaves me in some small doubt. We have it urged that *the fact alone* that the offender unlike the victim 'freely contributed to his situation' is of moral relevance. It is difficult to see what this relevance can be. One cannot but suspect that the objector is in one way or another so construing the case as to change it. He may, out of a kind of rooted habit, be persisting in the generally justified supposition that victims suffer more than offenders. He may have in mind some factor of a utilitarian kind so far unmentioned. The victimisation will involve a lying imputation of guilt. This lie, of course, is likely to bring a particular distress to the victim. Our case necessarily involves taking into account all such factors. Given all of them, it remains true that for other reasons the victim would experience no more distress than the offender. It is important, particularly so at this fundamental level of moral reflection, imaginatively to enter into this supposition. To do so, perhaps, one must have in mind features which might explain the unusual vulnerability of the offender. One must not tacitly suppress consideration of him and his situation. If one takes the case precisely as intended, is the fact alone that the offender unlike the victim did choose to offend one of moral relevance? I cannot see that it is. One may have considerably different attitudes to offender and victim, but they seem not to issue in specifiable moral reasons for action. If they were of such a kind as to do so, one would suspect more resistance to a claim that victimisation was preferable in a closely related case. I have in mind a choice between victimisation and punishment where, all things considered, the victim would experience somewhat less distress than the offender.

Our final conclusions are these. (1) Since, as we concluded at the beginning of this chapter, there are classes of offenders who are not deterred by the prospect of punishment, it cannot be acceptable that a society should attempt to prevent all offences by punishment alone. (2) Punishment cannot be justified by the argument alone that it is economically deterrent. If this and this alone were a sufficient justification, then the grossly unfair victimisation described in the section before this one would also be acceptable. This conclusion is not affected if we take into account what we have tended to ignore, that punishment may *incapacitate* a potential offender. (3) In anticipation of the discussion to come of compromise theories of punishment, we can say that punishment *may* be justified by being both economically deterrent and also deserved. To defend it as deserved, however, in so far as this is not to reiterate the claim that is economical of distress, is only to allude to the fact that it observes a certain principle of equality.

6. *Rule-Utilitarianism*

The deterrence theory of punishment is a logical consequence of the morality of utilitarianism. In rejecting it we reject that morality as well, one which may be cursorily expressed as the principle that an act is right or justified if it is likely to produce the best welfare-consequences: more satisfaction or at least less distress than any other act that might be performed instead. There is another morality, recently expounded although supposed to have been intended by Mill,[22] which is regarded as a form of utilitarianism. It is rule-utilitarianism and it would be claimed that it issues in a theory of punishment which would not justify the unacceptable victimisation we have imagined. Furthermore, the theory in question would apparently be regarded by some philosophers as that of economical deterrence. If these propositions are true, the argument of this chapter must be mistaken.

Rule-utilitarianism may be expressed as the principle that a particular action is right or justified if it is according to a rule which itself has a utilitarian justification, even if the action is likely to produce less satisfaction or more distress than some other action that is possible.[23] The principle is a result, in part, of reflection on punishment. Traditional utilitarianism, as we have seen, was thought to issue via the deterrence theory in the justification of certain victimisations, infractions of the rules of punishment. Victimisations were assumed always to be morally mistaken, and utilitarianism thus to be in question. Rule-utilitarianism has been regarded as a satisfactory alternative by those of the opinion that the rightness of conduct has to do only with the maximisation of satisfactions and the minimisation of distress. The rules of punishment were taken

22. See J. R. Urmson, 'The Interpretation of the Moral Philosophy of J. S. Mill', *Philosophical Quarterly*, 1953.

23. It is true, certainly, that traditional utilitarianism also makes use, rather puzzling use, of rules. What is certain is that the rules are guides and we are not enjoined to stick to them in all cases, no matter the consequences. For discussions of rule-utilitarianism see Urmson, *op. cit.*, J. Rawls, 'Two Concepts of Rules', *Philosophical Review*, 1955; J. J. C. Smart, 'Extreme and Restricted Utilitarianism', *Philosophical Quarterly*, 1956, H. J. Mc-Closkey, 'An Examination of Restricted Utilitarianism', *Philosophical Review*, 1957. Richard Brandt presents a justification of punishment in terms of rule-utilitarianism in *Ethical Theory* (Englewood Cliffs, N.J., 1969), Chapter Nineteen.

to have utilitarian justifications and therefore, given the new doctrine, to be inviolable. I wish to maintain two things, both of which seem obvious. Rule-utilitarianism is not a utilitarianism at all if one regards utilitarian moralities as those which have to do solely with satisfaction and distress, their maximisation and minimisation. Secondly, the theories of punishment in which it can issue are none of them the theory of deterrence.

Rule-utilitarianism is expressed, very vaguely, as the view that an action is right if it is according to a rule *which itself has a utilitarian justification*. What does this mean? What is it that justifies us in taking up a particular rule as something to follow even if doing so on a particular occasion will result in less satisfaction or more distress than is necessary? Let us have in the mind that rule or principle of equality which is infringed in the extreme case of victimisation where the victim's distress would be far greater than any distress to any particular individual if there were no victimisation. Can it be that we are to accept this rule because *usually* or *almost always* following it has the effect of producing more satisfaction or less distress? We can assume the latter to be true. It clearly does not provide a sufficient reason for accepting that we should *never* break the rule. Given *this* reason, why should we keep the rule on those occasions when breaking it would have the best welfare-consequences? Can it then be that we are to accept the rule because following it *always* has the best welfare-consequences? We know this isn't true. Indeed, the belief that certain victimisations would have the best welfare-consequences was precisely a reason for taking up rule-utilitarianism. These are the only possible grounds, in terms of best welfare-consequences alone, for adopting the rule in question. Neither has sufficient force. Whatever the ground for taking up the rule as always binding, it must involve more than a commitment to maximising satisfaction or minimising distress. It may involve, obviously, some fundamental commitment to equality. Also, of course, if the ensuing theory of punishment does involve an embargo on breaking the rule in question, it is not the deterrence theory. It is an attempt to justify punishment by reference to several values taken together.

3
Reform

1. *Punishment as Reformative*

THERE are a number of views which recommend particular practices for dealing with criminality on the grounds that they would reform or improve offenders, help them or 'socialise' them, and thereby reduce offences. Too often these doctrines are ill-defined or presented as group-orthodoxies beyond the need for explanation. They differ very considerably in character and assumptions. The traditional ones, but certainly not their successors, can be described as recommending the inculcation of moral principles. Some of them are so much concerned with the state of the offender as to give little attention to the prevention of offences. All of them, for different reasons, include rejections of retribution and deterrence. Of those to be mentioned here the first two recommend the practice of punishment while the others, which conceive of criminality as disorder or disability, recommend some practice of treatment. I shall have relatively little to say of any of them, partly for the reason that they are in a certain fundamental respect similar to the deterrence theory and so open to a familiar objection. The following chapter, however, is given over to consideration of the dogmas of freedom and determinism. The latter is a substantial part of conceptions of criminality as disorder or disability requiring treatment.

'Punishment is justified because it provides an opportunity for us to take steps to reform offenders and so to reduce offences.' It seems unlikely that anyone has ever believed punishment to be justified *solely* by the supposed fact that imprisoned men are morally improved and made law-abiding by chapel services, exhortatory chats, and regimens designed to build character. There has been a certain amount of faith in such things but those who have had it have been inclined to defend punishment by such other beliefs as that it is deserved. If one takes this first possible reformative doctrine by itself, it is open to casual dismissal. It is impossible to have anything remotely like conviction about the supposition that men are reformed by traditional ministrations or whatever and so become law-abiding. Furthermore, the conclusion which is claimed requires another premiss, a proposition that is indubitably false. What we are given is the premiss that certain steps may be taken which reform men and make them law-abiding, and the conclusion that punishment is justified because it enables us to take these steps. What needs to be established, of course, is that *only* punishment would give us the opportunity, or the best opportunity. This is false. It may be admitted that some form of control or restraint would be necessary if we were to attempt reformation in the suggested ways. This is not to say that we would have to *punish*. Punishment is a practice which aims to cause distress. A practice which does not have this feature is not punishment.

This latter difficulty is avoided by a doctrine of greater familiarity.[1] Here, it is punishment itself which is claimed to have a reformative effect.

It has this effect in several indirect ways. Punishment does deter men from breaking the law, and thus they are inclined to become habitually law-abiding. They do obey the law, but not from 'moral motives'. However, they are said to be more likely to advance from here than from elsewhere to a state in which they do obey the law from 'moral motives'. Secondly,

1. Dr. A. C. Ewing considers and defends such a view in *The Morality of Punishment* (London, 1929). It is more briefly stated in 'Punishment as a Moral Agency', *Mind*, 1927. Related accounts are given by J. M. E. McTaggart, *Studies in Hegelian Cosmology* (Cambridge, 1901), Chapter Five; Hastings Rashdall, *The Theory of Good and Evil* (London, 1907), Volume One, Chapter Nine; E. F. Carritt, *The Theory of Morals* (London, 1928), pp. 108–13. McTaggart, as I mentioned in the first chapter above, supposes Hegel to have held the view in question.

and more important, punishment may have the effect of emphasising to a man his immorality.

It is not only pain that is characteristic of punishment, it is pain inflicted because of wrong done and after a judicial decision involving a moral condemnation by an organ representing society. It is not only that the man suffers pain, but that he suffers as a consequence and sign of the condemnation of his act by society as immoral and pernicious. Now this surely is a striking way of bringing home to him, so far as external symbols can, the wickedness of his conduct. It is generally admitted that recognition of one's sin in some form or other is a necessary condition of real moral regeneration, and the formal and impressive condemnation by society involved in punishment is an important means toward bringing about this recognition on the part of the offender.[2]

Thirdly, punishment has a moral effect on individuals other than those who actually experience it.

If it may help the offender to realise the badness of his action, may it not help others to realise the badness before they have committed the kind of action in question at all? This must not be confused with a purely deterrent effect. A man who abstains from crime just because he is deterred abstains through fear of suffering and not because he thinks it wicked; a man who abstains because the condemnation of the crime by society and the State has brought its wickedness home to him abstains from moral motives and not merely from fear of unpleasant consequences to himself.[3]

The second and third propositions do not precisely rest on the mistake that members of a society could or would not regard offences as wrongful without the demonstration of punishment. They do rest on some such assumptions as this one, that if an

2. Ewing, *The Morality of Punishment*, p. 97.
3. *Ibid.*, p. 96.

action is not one that is punished by the state, individuals may not realise the extent of its wrongfulness. We are said[4] to be inclined to allocate wrongful actions to two classes: those that may sometimes be excused and those that are absolutely prohibited. When an action is made a crime, and those who commit it are punished, the effect is to firmly locate it in the second class.

Punishment, then, is both a deterrent and an effective condemnation, and as such it has reformative consequences. It contributes to a change in the beliefs of offenders and others as to the wrongfulness of certain actions. It thereby contributes to a change for the better in behaviour. A good many things may be said about and against these claims. What is advanced is certainly a considerably simplified conception of the relationships between morality and the practice of punishment. It seems fairly evident that an effective creation of criminal law, in the societies with which we are familiar, usually depends upon an already existing consensus as to the wrongfulness or undesirability of certain behaviour. It cannot be in general true that the making of an action into an offence results in a moral reallocation of the kind suggested. In certain cases, no doubt, making an action into an offence serves to increase and fortify beliefs as to its immorality. I wish, however, to avoid a difficult and inessential discussion of the relations between punishment and accepted morality. Let us suppose the existence of a society, very different from ours, where punishment does contribute greatly to law abidance by influencing beliefs and attitudes as to the immorality of offences. The suggestion we are considering is that punishment would here be justified *solely* by these effects. This can be shown to be mistaken in precisely the way in which the deterrence theory has been shown to be mistaken. To accept a principle to the effect that punishment would be justified solely in virtue of its influence on moral beliefs and the further consequences in behaviour would be to commit oneself to unacceptable victimisations. No doubt it would be difficult to conceive of a victimisation in which the victim was led to morality and lawfulness. His victimisation might be justified, none the less, by its effects on others. Given

4. *Ibid.*

the unacceptability of this victimisation, the conclusion would follow that even in the imagined society punishment could not be justified by the suggested principle of reformation alone.

The deterrence theory, according to the argument, fails because it places insufficient limitation on what may be done in order to secure certain behaviour. It fails to take into account a limitation having to do with equality of treatment. This principle is observed, it seems, by our practice of punishment. The doctrine we are presently considering fails because it places insufficient limitation on what may be done in order to secure changes in belief and attitude and consequent behaviour. It does not take into account a feature of our practice of punishment which is essential to any justification it may have. What would have to be true in order for the present doctrine to escape the objection? That in any conceivable situation we would prefer (1) a course of action which would result in certain moral beliefs and lawfulness to (2) a course of action having other results. This, I take it, can be shown to be false. To do so would require both a detailed development of the doctrine and also a repetition of essentially the sequence of argument of the last chapter.[5]

There is also a special objection to this doctrine and to others like it. If we attempt to deter by punishment, our intention is to affect behaviour, but not by changing certain beliefs and attitudes. If we attempt to reform by punishment, the changing of beliefs and attitudes is an end in itself as well as a means to fewer offences. But just what will be the consequences if we succeed? What will be the consequences if we change the beliefs and attitudes of members of society with respect to certain actions? Those who are quick to suppose that a great deal will be gained usually make the assumption, so evident in the quoted passages above, that whatever is punished at present is certainly wrong. They assume, that is, that punishment will always create or reinforce attitudes that certainly are

5. Ewing attempts some rejoinders to the traditional claims about victimisation. His rejoinders rest, in my view, on a happy choice of cases. See *The Morality of Punishment*, p. 90 ff.

right. This is simple error. The history of the law is littered with
moral barbarities. At *any* time, indeed, the law includes
elements which are open to question. What is required, with
respect to these elements, is not that members of society should
be influenced in some direction by the practice of punishment.
What is desirable, rather, is both that the law as it stands be
obeyed, and that there be unrestrained discussion of the issues
in dispute. Such discussion, after all, gives us the best assur-
ance we can have of rational decisions and moral progress.
Discussion should not be impeded, with respect to the issues in
question, by a practice of punishment that coerces judgement
in one direction. One might then maintain that given a choice
between punishment of a reformative kind and punishment of
a deterrent kind, where the preventive effect would be the
same, the deterrent punishment would be preferable.

Someone may object at this point that there cannot be any
doubt about the moral correctness of some core of the law.
Would it not be a good thing if at least certain offences were
regarded by more people as wholly wrong? We are here in the
neighbourhood of a number of considerable difficulties, including the ancient problem of the moral agent. Out of what grounds
does the good man act? What is suggested to us by the theory
of punishment we are considering is that one takes an important
step on the way to becoming such a man by being impressed
by the condemnations of others. It is not, of course, that one
is impressed by their reasons or their arguments, but rather by
the declarations in which they issue. These are punishments.
But surely this is not a way to becoming a good man. Surely
I am most admirable as a moral agent if I obey the law out
of a sympathetic and impartial awareness of the effects on
others of its being broken. My first major step toward this
state will involve an awareness of the victims of offences
rather than the condemnation of offenders.

2. *Illness and Treatment*

'Those who break the law do so as a consequence of illness
and so we should treat them rather than punish them.' These

judgements are expressed or implied in a good many books but not, I think, satisfactorily explained or defended.[6] The inherent assumptions are that the mental illness or disability, however conceived, is as much a matter of discovery and description as physical illness, and that it explains and excuses criminal actions. Punishment, almost invariably regarded as necessarily retributive in character, is thought to be out of the question. All of this, needless to say, while orthodoxy to some, is questioned or denied by other psychiatrists and psychologists concerned with the law.

It seems an obvious truth, and one worth remembering, that the influence on the law of the social studies, medicine, psychology, and also certain theories of personal development, has been humanising and entirely beneficial. That we now do less punishing and more of other things is in accord with discoveries made in these inquiries and the recommendations associated with them. None of the traditional theories of punishment or at least none of the associated beliefs about the numbers of people who rightly may be punished can avoid serious emendation at the hands of psychiatrists, sociologists, and others. That we should, because of their evidence, do even less punishing and more of other things seems a likelihood. Should we, however, give up punishment entirely and substitute treatment? Are all offenders ill? Whether or not one thinks so, of course, depends on one's conception of illness.

In English law, from 1843 until 1957, the McNaghten rules provided a specification of mental abnormality: the abnormality required as a defence against a criminal charge. As we have noticed already, for a man to have been mentally abnormal in this sense, with respect to a particular act, he must at the time have suffered as a consequence of disease of the mind from a defect of reason such that he did not know the nature of his act or that it was wrong. The 'diseases of the mind' in question are traditional madnesses or incapabilities, or some of them. Not to know the nature of one's act, in this context, is for example not to know that what one is attacking is a human

6. For an analysis see A. G. N. Flew, 'Crime or Disease', *The British Journal of Sociology*, 1954.

body. A wrong act is taken to be an illegal act. Clearly enough, given a conception of mental illness based on the McNaghten rules, one would be a long way indeed from the generalisation that all offenders are mentally ill. The rules, certainly, have since their inception been criticised as too narrow. In the main, this narrowness consists in regarding a man as sane who knows what he is doing, and that it is wrong, but lacks the emotional capacity even to begin to act in any other way. Such men, it is said, are often obviously and classically mad and it is absurd that they should be held responsible for actions which are the consequence of their illness. In 1957 a relatively trivial step toward widening the English legal conception of mental abnormality took place. In other countries there have long been much wider conceptions.

One might try at this point to arrive at a more inclusive idea of illness by putting aside consideration of the law and its history and turning directly to the doctors, or to some doctors.[7] Abnormal mental life, we are told, although endlessly various, can be divided into forms of illness which are dependent on some distinct bodily disorder and forms of illness which are identified at the psychological rather than the physical level and for which organic causes have not yet been isolated. In the first group are to be found dementia and also the various forms of mental defectiveness. The confusion, delirium, and loss of intellectual capability that is typical of states of dementia may result from physical sickness, injury, kinds of intoxication, inheritances. The forms of mental retardation, including idiocy, imbecility, and feeble-mindedness, are also of known physical basis.

As for the second group of conditions, it can be broken down into a number of categories, the first of which takes in disorders of emotion. Central here are states of anxiety, of depression, and of mania. A second category includes schizophrenic states, marked by disordered thinking, emotional excesses and incongruities, hallucinations, odd or bizarre conduct. A third category includes states of obsession and compulsion, various forms of hysterical illness, and also

7. My sketch is taken from David Stafford-Clark, *Psychiatry Today* (Harmondsworth, 1952).

psychopathic states. Among psychopaths one finds a significant number of offenders, recidivists in particular.

None the less, given even a determination to expand the notions of this schema, it seems fairly clear that not all offenders can be regarded as falling under it. If this is the extent of sickness, not all offenders are sick. This, of course, is the attitude of many medical authorities. If a man is to be regarded as mentally ill or incapacitated, he must exhibit some established syndrome, where 'established' means something like 'included in standard textbooks of psychiatry'.

There remain other possibilities. One can begin with one of the related but competing theories of personal development and arrive at a host of disorders. I have in mind those theories of which Freud's is the exemplar. It encompasses, among its fundamental concepts, those of the unconscious mind, basic instinctual drives, such early sexual phases as the anal-sadistic, sublimation, and repression, the Oedipus conflict and its resolution, the pleasure principle and the reality principle, the formation of the Super-Ego. It would be pointless to attempt any encapsulation of the theory. Given it, one can display the actions of offenders as consequences of emotional states which are themselves the results of deviations from a normal course of development.[8] Offenders, it may be said, are individuals suffering from character disorders, and these consist in faulty relationships between Id, Ego, and Super-Ego. Mainly because of unsatisfactory emotional environments or simply inconsistent treatment in early life, no adequate Super-Ego or conscience has been developed. Offenders are like children whose instinctual drives for immediate gratification have not come under control. Or, it may be said of some individuals that their experience of the Oedipus conflict was not satisfactorily resolved and they have been left with an ungovernable reaction to figures of authority and indeed authority in any form. Alternatively, some men may be offending because they desire punishment. The feeling of guilt which issues in this desire may have its origin in early sexual experience. Or, a

8. See, for example, Kate Friedlander, *The Psycho-Analytical Approach to Juvenile Delinquency* (London, 1947).

man's behaviour may be explained by the fact that there was
no successful emergence from the stage of anal-sadism, or by
the fact that through a certain experience he has regressed to
that stage. Or again, it may be said that an individual has
become fixated in that common illusion of children, the family
romance, and steals in order to try to maintain it.

Whatever else may be said of the enterprise, the notions of
the theory seem to be such as to allow it to be put to very
wide use. It is not obvious that it cannot be applied to all
offenders. Rather it is a matter of argument whether all offenders, or perhaps all but some of those who are mentally ill in
the traditional sense, suffer from personality or character
disabilities resulting from abnormal emotional development.
There are also related doctrines which offer at least the possibility of general application. Some of them are found attractive
for their relatively common-sensical air. It is supposed by a
good many people that there is a causal connection between
anti-social conduct and separation from one's mother in infancy
or rejection by her, or loss of affection.[9] One or more of these
experiences gives rise to a personality disorder and it in turn
produces criminal behaviour.

There is another less familiar alternative to be found in a
strictly physical account of personal development.[10] Here too
there are inherent dangers of disorder and its consequences.
We are reminded, for example, that when an external stimulus
excites a sensory surface of the body, excitation is passed on
through synapses to the brain and then to other parts of the
body. There is also inhibition, which is a kind of resistance to
excitation. These two processes enter into another one which
is of fundamental importance to the individual's development.
This is conditioning, the process of establishing responses to
stimuli. If a puff of air is directed at the cornea of a man's eye,
he blinks. If he hears a particular sound each time he feels a
puff, then, after sound and puff have occurred together a number of times, a conditioned reflex is established. That is, some

9. For a careful discussion of these theories, see Wootton, *Social Science
and Social Pathology*, Chapter Four.
10. See H. J. Eysenck, *Crime and Personality* (London, 1964).

percentage of times when he hears the sound and there is no puff, he blinks. The extent to which the reflex is established may be said to be determined by the degree of inhibition of his nervous system and the number of times he has experienced sound and puff together. *As with the development of the blink-response, so with human behaviour in general.* A child misbehaves in a particular way and is then punished in some way. His response to the punishment is fear and pain. By a process of conditioning exactly parallel to that one which produced the blink-response, he comes to respond with something like fear and pain to misbehaving itself. After some repetitions, the response is sufficiently strong to result in the child's avoiding the behaviour in question to some particular extent. This is a matter of conditioning, not a making of conscious choices.

Not all individuals who have nervous systems of such kinds that they condition badly become offenders. Two other requirements must be satisfied before it becomes a probability or better that a particular child will come to break the law. It is also a consequence of inheritance that an individual be of a certain degree of emotionality or neuroticism. He has a place on a personality scale. Persons at one extreme of the scale, who are very high in emotionality, have such qualities as aggressiveness, restlessness, moodiness. Persons at the other extreme are likely to be calm, reliable, carefree. A high degree of emotionality in the suggested sense is the second condition of criminality. The third is environment and in particular childhood punishments and disapprovals. Criminality, then, is reducible to conditionability, emotionality, and 'input'. If the possibility of certain other factors is sometimes mentioned by behavioural psychologists, it is not seriously considered. Certainly there is no room for free decisions as usually conceived. 'The deduction which may be made from our general theory is relatively uncompromising. We would regard behaviour from a completely deterministic point of view; that is to say, the individual's behaviour is determined completely by his heredity and by the environmental influences which have been brought to bear on him.'[11]

11. *Ibid*, p. 177.

There are still other ways in which criminality may be described and explained in terms of disorder or incapability. 'Deviant syndromes' are explained by sociologists as primarily a consequence of environment rather than individual development. Offenders, on one view, simply have acquired the common pattern of behaviour of the neighbourhood or of some peer group. 'When persons become criminal, they do so because of contacts with criminal patterns and also because of isolation from anti-criminal patterns.'[12] They, like everyone else, have norms imposed upon them. The norms in question happen not to call for obedience to the law, or to some laws. Indeed, they sometimes call for infractions. With respect both to this and the other kinds of explanation, incidentally, it is not always true that the supposed sickness or disorder or disability is thought to *give rise to* criminal behaviour. Rather, there is an evident tendency to regard the behaviour itself as the sickness, disorder, or disability. To be mentally healthy is to behave in certain ways; to be unhealthy is to break the law or to act in other anti-social ways.[13] It will then be pointless to attempt to explain the behaviour by the disability, but not pointless to try to explain the behaviour, whether or not conceived as a disability, by some independent factor or factors, perhaps the social environment.

Finally, of course, there are some combinations of these several doctrines. Offenders are what they are, it may be said, as a consequence of both personal and social factors. One might try to explain a man's becoming a criminal in terms both of Freudian categories and the sociologist's notion of anomie. It seems possible that something like a spirit of compromise is growing among psychologists, sociologists, and others who concern themselves with the theory of criminality. It has not grown so far, to my knowledge, as to produce fruits. There has recently also been more emphasis on particular kinds of offenders and an increasing unwillingness to regard criminal behaviour as homogeneous stuff. Full-time thieves are very different from rapists and both of them are quite unlike the man who

12. Edwin H. Sutherland, *Principles of Criminology* (Chicago, 1955), p. 78.
13. See *Social Science and Social Pathology*, Chapter Seven.

G

assaults the neighbour who has been annoying him for years.[13a]

Several of the general doctrines, of course, are conjoined with quite specific recommendations as to treatment. If offenders are suffering from disabilities which are to be explained in a Freudian way, then it seems that psychoanalysis or psychotherapy is indicated. Often, for clear reasons, one finds a reluctance to propose such a treatment system. It is difficult to see an alternative, however, given the usual condemnations of punishment as barbarous or useless, a dismissal of the utility of other kinds of treatment, and the acceptance that we should try to prevent offences. On the other hand, if offences are importantly the result of unsuccessful conditioning, or successful conditioning of an anti-social kind, then behaviour-therapy is presumably the answer or a major part of it. A shoe-fetishist may now be so conditioned that the sight of a shoe in certain circumstances, far from exciting him, produces nausea or terror. The same procedure could be attempted with all anti-social behaviour. We might also take steps to alter the conditionability of individuals. Something of this kind, involving the use of drugs, has been attempted with delinquent boys. Finally, whatever steps we choose to take later in their lives, we might consider the desirability of testing the conditionability of school children. 'Once this particular aspect of the child's nature was known, we could . . . pick out those who, by virtue of their poor conditionability, are predestined to become criminals and delinquents, and recommend to their parents a kind of upbringing that would minimise that possibility.'[14] There are, needless to say, other recommendations as to treatment attached to other diagnoses. Those who are impressed by the argument that offenders are the products of maternal deprivation sometimes advocate particular kinds of institution, unlike prisons, where individuals can come to a kind of maturation earlier denied them. Finally, there are the

13a. A valuable essay on general theories of crime and their weaknesses, and an argument for particularised research, is to be found in Wootton, *Crime and the Criminal Law* (London, 1963), Chapter One.

14. Eysenck, *op. cit.*, p. 163.

less doctrinaire proposals to the effect that we should establish a treatment system comprising within it approaches of various kinds.

3. *Objections*

Great numbers of questions, most of them not open to settlement here, are raised by these doctrines. Consider, for a start, these three propositions, each of which has been asserted or at least implied. (1) All offenders, perhaps save some of the traditionally mad, are suffering from personality or character disorders resulting from a certain abnormal emotional development, and these disorders are the main causes of their behaviour. (2) All offenders, perhaps save some of the traditionally mad, are the products of certain processes of conditioning, and their behaviour is to be mainly explained in this way. (3) All offenders, again excluding some of the traditionally mad, offend mainly because they have been formed by a certain social environment. One might attempt to trim, amend, or interpret these propositions in various ways in order to make them consistent. If they are taken as they often have been intended, however, two at least of them must be false.

It is difficult to resist certain familiar suspicions about the first one, either if offenders are presented as the consequences of unsatisfactory relations between Id, Ego, and Super-Ego or if they are explained in terms of more particular hypotheses of a Freudian kind. General questions about psycho-analytic theory raise themselves. Without being drawn into the ideological conflicts between the analytical movements and their critics, one can question the nature and the extent of the evidence for the propositions put forward. One can also question the precision of the concepts at the base of the system. One can discard a number of worn defensive strategies, including the simple rejoinder that each criticism of psycho-analytic theory may be regarded as no more than resistance, in the technical sense. As for the second proposition, that one based on the notion of conditioning, it would seem best taken as a simplification of some hypothesis yet to be clarified and tested. Here again, for good reasons, there is controversy among those who are engaged in the relevant disciplines. One good reason is that the theory flattens out what seem to be striking differences. At least certain human decisions, whatever phenomena they are, appear to be very different from blink-responses. Finally, with respect to the more testable assertions of the sociologists, let us notice only that again there is extensive disagreement among those most qualified to judge and that the explanatory power of a number of familiar sociological claims is in doubt. It is difficult to accept, as a complete account of why some individuals offend, that they were members of a certain group, class, or society.

To mention these problems is simply to draw attention to what is certainly a fact. It cannot be regarded as anything like settled that *any* of the three propositions, or more discriminating versions of them, is true. It seems likely that each of them represents human behaviour by way of a too-simple and distorting model. Nor can the efficacy of different modes of treatment be regarded as established. I shall not attempt any adjudication or, of course, any speculation as to a less doctrinaire theory. Instead, I should like to notice some difficulties that will have to be faced by *any* such theory and its attendant recommendations as to treatment. I take these difficulties to be insuperable. Before mentioning them, let us be clearer about the doctrine we are anticipating. It will be distinguished, first, by a denial of free choice as ordinarily conceived. This is what is common to the views of criminality as sickness or disability enumerated above. The practice recommended in place of punishment, secondly, will be one of treatment, a practice in which characters, personalities, views, or attitudes are changed as a means to changing behaviour. These changes would not be brought about by what I shall call argument, or not wholly so. What will be the claimed justification? It will be that the practice recommended in place of punishment would in some way improve offenders and in that way prevent offences. The claim will be, in so far as the doctrine is of the single-principle kind we are at present discussing, that this in itself is sufficient to justify the practice.

One difficulty in accepting such a doctrine would be that one

would be committed to what we may persist in calling victimisation. Hitherto, we have understood victimisations to be
departures from rules which govern our practice of punishment.
It might then be said that one could not possibly have a
victimisation within a treatment system. Let us extend the
notion far enough to cover impositions of distress not in accord
with principles of equality. Clearly enough, one could have
victimisations in this sense. Someone may now object, on
another ground, that one could not have victimisation as a
consequence of a doctrine of treatment rather than punishment.
The ground may be the supposition that treatment cannot be
against the will of the patient. This is not a logical truth, obviously, and in many circumstances unlikely to be a truth at all.
It is mere utopianism to suppose that if punishment were
replaced by treatment, of whatever effective kind, offenders
would cheerfully present themselves for their remedies. The
only realistic alternative to punishment, of the kind in question,
would be a *coercive* system of treatment. With coercion one gets
the element of possible victimisation which was thought to be
missing. One also gets an answer, incidentally, to one quite
different objection that might be made against a treatment
system of the kind we are considering. It might be objected,
familiarly, that such a system would perhaps help offenders but
would not sufficiently prevent offences. That is, it might change
known offenders by treatment but it would not influence
others against offending. The supposition is that the prospect of
being treated would not be deterrent. For several reasons having
to do with the fact that treatment would be enforced on
individuals, this seems a mistake.

To return to the main point, however, it seems obvious that
a medical authority might impose too much distress on an
individual either in the interest of curing him or improving
his condition, or in the interest of that and of preventing
offences. That, at any rate, would be a possible consequence if
the practice in question was governed only by some principle
to the effect that treatment was justified if successful in securing
such ends. It is such a practice and principle that we are at
present discussing. If a practice of treatment was established,

and it did exclude victimisations, one would have to accept that any justification it had was not simply that offenders were treated and offences prevented.

A second difficulty would have to do with the changing of beliefs or attitudes mainly by means other than the giving of reasons. The general argument against other means is that there are safeguards of the first importance in maintaining the place or rather the places in society of rational discussion. The effects of what may be called indoctrination are likely to be felt far beyond the area in which it is used. It is entirely mistaken to say[15] that our present practice of punishment succeeds in indoctrination or attempts to indoctrinate. What it primarily attempts to do is to change behaviour. It might reasonably be pointed out, on the other hand, that we certainly do influence children by other than rational means. This is so, and to some extent defensible. It might also be admitted that in certain cases behaviour-therapy for adults is justifiable, even against the wishes of the individuals in question. These would be cases in which there was a danger of very great harm to particular individuals and no other more tolerable way of avoiding it. It certainly does not follow that society could justifiably treat all law-breakers or potential law-breakers in this way.

There is also a question of the allocation of a society's resources. One sometimes has the feeling that for reformists no expenditure could be too great if it secured an insignificant incidence of criminality. It is as if there was no question but that an army of psycho-analysts would be best engaged in dealing with those who commit criminal offences, about half of which are motoring offences. Surely the claims of other sectors and institutions in society must be considered. Should we have so many psychoanalysts or practitioners of whatever kind? If so, what numbers of them should be concerned in, say, the education of children rather than criminality? Our practice of punishment is often said to be inefficient and wasteful. If we are far indeed from having it, there remains a possibility that a radically different system would be inefficient and wasteful

15. Eysenck, *op. cit.,* p. 173.

in different ways. One can certainly conceive of two societies such that one with a higher incidence of criminality would be far preferable.

Finally, with respect to the doctrine we are anticipating, it will involve the denial that offenders are free in their offences and responsible for them. If it is anything like those doctrines we already have, it will involve a quite general thesis of determinism. It will not be allowed that *anyone* chooses or acts freely, in an ordinary sense of the word, or is to be held responsible. For several reasons this large and all too enduring question calls for fuller consideration.

4
Freedom

1. *Freedom and Punishment*

THE justification of punishment in terms of retribution pre-
supposes that men sometimes make free choices for which they
are responsible. Indeed, as we have seen, the claim that a man
deserves a penalty for an action may best be taken to mean, in
part, that he was free in the action and responsible for it.
The retribution theory, then, could not survive a demonstration
of the truth of determinism. Our main objection to that defence
of punishment was of a moral kind. If men were never free and
responsible, in certain common senses of the words, there would
also exist an insuperable objection to retributivism of a non-
evaluative kind. The deterrence theory is not in the same way
bound up with the controversy about human freedom. Quite
commonly the holders of the theory have been advocates of
some doctrine of determinism. They have argued, by way of it,
against retributivism. It is clear, though, that determinism is
not a presupposition of their own justification of punishment
in the way in which freedom is a presupposition of retributivism.
Punishment might be justified in virtue of being an economical
deterrent even if determinism was false. If it is true, of course,
and retributivism thus unacceptable, the field is left to the
supposed justifications in terms of deterrence and reform. In
connection with the latter we have just seen that conceptions
of criminality as disorder or disability are in ways determinist.
Furthermore, the truth of determinism would provide at least
a retort against a major criticism of the associated recommendations that we treat and not punish offenders. Let me say for

the moment, simply, that the distinction between rational argument and indoctrination may be thought to be put in danger by determinism.

In the chapter following this one, we shall consider justifications of punishment in terms of several principles. These typically contain a retributivist argument and thus, like traditional retributivism, presuppose human freedom. Finally, it seems to me at least arguable that advocacy of all these doctrines about punishment, traditional and recent, requires an assumption of freedom in quite another way. The same is true of what I shall suggest is the best that can be said for the practice of punishment. For all these reasons the subject can do with attention. This chapter, none the less, gives it rather more than the central intention of the book requires. This indulgence on my part, I hope, will be found worth while. What will be said is in certain respects unfamiliar.

2. Determinism

A number of philosophers who have considered the ordinary belief in human freedom have concluded that there is no opposing case to be met. They have held, that is, that there is no intelligible or coherent doctrine of determinism. This easy way with a problem is open to the easy and sufficient reply that we as much lack an intelligible and coherent account of what it is, or would be, to choose or decide freely. However, determinism *is* unclear and any discussion must begin with some examination or stipulation of the *meaning* of the claim that all or some events are the products of preceding causes. What is it for one thing to cause another?

Let us first put aside the central use of the word 'cause' in ordinary life. We say that the cause of a man's showing irritation was that he was ignored or that a house caught fire because there wasn't a screen in front of a fireplace, that someone couldn't find an address because of not knowing London and being unable to find a taxi, that the war went on because members of a government were entranced by an ideology. In each case, the cause would not by itself bring about the effect.

It was necessary to the fire, for example, that the floor in front of the fireplace was inflammable, that there was oxygen in the room, and so on. Talk of a cause in this sense, then, is talk of *one* of a set of factors which only together are sufficient to give rise to an effect. Why do we single out one particular factor or condition and call it the cause? Reflection on the examples will give the beginning of an answer. At least often, one factor is singled out because it is the only human action or human failure involved. At other times, one factor is chosen because, within a certain context or given certain expectations, it is abnormal or unusual.[1]

To say that all actions are caused, in this sense, may be to make a philosophically uncontroversial remark. To say in this way that someone was caused to write a book on some subject by some fact about his personality or his finances is not to say that his conduct was unfree. Another equally important factor may have been that he willingly chose, every so often, to go on with it. We may use the word 'cause' in other and more consequential ways, to refer to some part or the whole of the set of factors which give rise to an effect. It is the latter use that is important at present. The cause of a particular event, in this sense, is that set of factors sufficient to produce it. Their specification is a matter of considerable difficulty. One may say, however, that the cause in this sense of the house's catching fire was the set of conditions including the absence of a fire-screen in front of a fireplace, an ember's falling from the grate, its resting on a wooden floor for a certain time and the presence of oxygen. This description may be criticised both as incomplete and as inclusive of redundancies. What is unlikely to be disputed is that *some* set of conditions was sufficient to produce the effect. But what more can be said of the relationship between such a cause and its effect? This is the traditional problem of causation and one important source of the unclarity of determinism. We are likely to say that given the existence of a cause in this sense, the effect is *certain* to follow or that it *must*

1. This ordinary sense of 'cause' is closely related to the legal sense, which is carefully discussed in H. L. A. Hart and A. M. Honoré, *Causation in the Law* (Oxford, 1959).

follow. We may say that it *necessarily* follows. What relationship of necessity is this? It is not, of course, logical necessity. To assert of a particular set of conditions that it did not produce what in fact was its effect is to fall into error but not self-contradiction. Nor do we know truths about causes and effects without recourse to experience.

Hume and his many followers, of course, maintain there is *no* relationship of necessity whatever between causes and effects. To return to the example of the fire, we have a set of conditions or what I shall sometimes call a circumstance, C, and the event of the house's catching fire, E. What may be said of C and E, according to the Humean account, is only that C preceded E, that they were contiguous in space and time, and that circumstances similar to C are always related in these several ways to events similar to E. Circumstances like C, in the familiar phrase, are *constantly conjoined* with events like E. When we say that C caused E we can sensibly mean no more than this. Indeed, this is what we do mean. The traditional objection is that this cannot be so, since there are instances of constant conjunction that are not acceptable as instances of cause and effect.

A particular day is followed by a particular night and the two together constitute an instance of constant conjunction: days are always followed by nights. However, we do not regard the day in question as the cause of the night. There is no point in remarking, incidentally, that 'day' and' night' may be given scientific definitions such that we *would* accept that days cause nights.[2] In the intended sense, it may be said, the day in question is a period of light on a part of the earth's surface. The night is a period of darkness. This day and night are an instance of a constant conjunction and would, if the account we are considering was correct, be cause and effect. A second objection is that the given account makes all causal statements in a way general. Certainly we may use 'cause' and 'effect' to refer to classes of things. It is also common, as we have seen,

2. The remark is by Moritz Schlick, 'Causality in Everyday Life and Recent Science', *Readings in Philosophical Analysis* (New York, 1949), edited by Herbert Feigl and Wilfrid Sellars, p. 517.

to use them to refer to particulars: a certain circumstance or set of conditions and a certain event, each with one place in space and time. On the given account of the language of causation, I do more than mention two particulars when I say that one was the cause of the other. To say that C caused E is to say that C happened and then the contiguous event E happened, and circumstances like C are always so related to events like E. This seems unlikely.

Defenders of the Humean account of causation have generally attempted to meet the first objection by maintaining that the supposed non-causal instances of constant conjunction are not really instances of constant conjunction in the intended sense. It has sometimes been explained that a class of circumstances is to be regarded as constantly conjoined with a class of events only if these situations and events have always been conjoined in the past and also *always will be*. This is ambiguous. It may be taken to mean something such that the proposed account of causation would still commit us to regarding a day as the cause of a night. This would happen if we were of the opinion that days will in fact always be followed by nights. What seems sometimes to be intended in such an amendment is something like this: a class of circumstances and a class of events are to be regarded as constantly conjoined if they *would* continue to be conjoined even if certain things in the universe were to change. More particularly, an event of the kind in question would occur, given that a circumstance of the kind in question obtained, *no matter what else was true*.[3] Given some such explanation, it can be argued that yesterday and last night are not an instance of a constant conjunction. The occurrence of a particular day would *not* be followed by a night if the earth were to stop rotating. If we take an undoubted causal connection, on the other hand, it does satisfy this definition of constant conjunction. Take, for example, that circumstance which we do regard as the cause of a particular day. It will have among its factors the rotation of the earth and the burning of

3. Cf. John Watling, 'Propositions Asserting Causal Connection', *Analysis*, 1953, and Peter Downing, 'Levels of Discourse', Ph.D. Dissertation, University of London, 1959.

the sun. Given the obtaining of a circumstance of *this* kind, whatever else was true, a day would occur.

By some such means one can move toward accommodating the objection. Doing so, of course, involves a radical amendment or indeed a rejection of Hume's view. What we now have is this. To say a particular circumstance was the cause of an event is to say that the obtaining of the circumstance preceded and was contiguous with the event, that similar events are always so conjoined with similar circumstances, and that given such a circumstance an event of the kind in question would occur no matter what else was the case. Obviously, this faces the second objection, in that all causal statements are presented as general. However, we can preserve the strength of the account, and not open it to any new objections, if we simply drop the curious reference to circumstances and events other than the single pair with which we are primarily concerned. We can drop the supposition that causal statements refer to whole classes of circumstances and events. We may say, simply, that to say that C caused E is to say that E followed C and that when C obtained E would have followed whatever else was true. No doubt we believe more than this when we assert a causal connection between two particulars, but there is no good reason for thinking that this belief is part of the content of what we assert. We need not think that what may be regarded as evidence for the causal assertion, a general belief about the conjunction of circumstances and events, is *part of* the assertion.

There will be a reluctance to accept this account of what we mean when we say that some circumstance was the cause of an event. Do we really mean, partly, that given the obtaining of the circumstance, the event would have followed *whatever else was the case*? Do we intend so strong a claim? Someone may say that we merely mean, rather, that the circumstances obtained and the event followed, the circumstance being sufficient to produce the event. It seems that if we do mean this, we are also committed to the seemingly stronger claim. We have the idea of a set of conditions sufficient *by itself* to give rise to an event. If it *is* sufficient, we would get the same result if everything else was different save that the set of conditions did

100 PUNISHMENT: THE SUPPOSED JUSTIFICATIONS

obtain. To suppose that E would not follow C if 'attendant circumstances' were in some way different and unfavourable is to suppose that C is *not* sufficient to give rise to E.

There remain a number of extremely difficult problems. What analysis can be given of a statement that given a certain circumstance an effect *would* have followed whatever else happened? Or, to choose another formulation I shall use, how are we to analyse the statement that given a certain circumstance, nothing other than a particular effect *could* have followed, whatever else happened? One cannot ignore these demands for explanation, certainly, if one's intention is to treat adequately of the problem of causation. My different intention has been to give a sketch of an account of what is meant by causal claims. It is, I suggest, sufficiently intelligible to provide one of the bases for further discussion. Certainly the causal relationship has not been finally clarified. It cannot be said, however, that it remains so obscure as to make useful discussion of determinism impossible. There are also other problems and obscurities, some of which attach only to forms of determinism other than the one upon which I shall concentrate. I allude below to some of those which are relevant but others must go unnoticed. None, I think, is insuperable: determinism can at least be adequately formulated.[4]

Are all human choices, decisions and actions caused? Is each of them a *necessary consequent* of some antecedent circumstance? Is it true of each, that is, that it could not have been otherwise no matter what else happened, given a certain circumstance? Is each element of each circumstance also a necessary consequent itself? In the past those who have given an affirmative answer to these questions have often derived it from the Law of Causation, that all events without exception are caused. The inductive support for this major premiss is that multitudes of *physical* events, events not particularly related to human choice and action, do have causes. The whole argument, then, proceeds from knowledge of one kind of event to a claim about

4. I do not mean to imply that there are no useful senses of 'cause' other than the two mentioned or that only a determinism based on the sense just set out poses a problem for human freedom.

events of a very different kind. For this reason, it inspires something less than confidence. Physical and mental events are of different categories, as we are so often reminded, and at least caution is required in considering whether what is true of the former is also true of the latter. More contemporary determinism avoids this and other difficulties. It is argued that some mental events can be shown to be caused, and that this is a sufficient basis for an extrapolation to the conclusion that all choices and decisions are caused. One line of argument here, of which we have already seen something, begins from the claim that some mental events can be shown to be consequences of mental causes. Rather more coercive for several reasons is the argument which begins from the premiss that some mental events have been shown to have *physical* causes. Over the past decade or two, there have been striking advances in neuro-physiological knowledge. It is nowhere near true, of course, that causal accounts of a physical kind have been given of the mental events in which we are most interested. That is, there has been no specific causal explanation, in terms, say, of the firing of neurons in the brain, for choices and decisions. To get to the conclusion that these are physically caused, a considerable extrapolatory step is required. What is true is that causal connections are established between other mental phenomena and chemical and electrical events and states in the brain. The possibility of producing feelings of ease, relaxation, joy, satisfaction, irritation, fear, or pain by electrical stimulation of brain centres is fairly familiar. There are established neuro-physiological procedures for the alteration of states of mental illness. Memory has also been the subject of considerable investigation and a kind of sequential and detailed experiencing of past events has been produced recurrently by electrical stimulation of the cortex. Finally, to mention a different order of support for determinism, growing knowledge in the field of cybernetics has established that complex logical operations can be reduced to steps that can be carried out by relatively simple mechanisms.[5]

5. A useful layman's summary of recent research of the kind mentioned in this paragraph, together with bibliographies, can be found in *The Machinery of the Brain* (New York, 1963), by Dean E. Wooldridge.

The ever-increasing number of such facts, which have analogues in quite ordinary experience, does seem to pose a threat to ordinary beliefs about choice and responsibility. It is difficult to resist the feeling that there is some considerable warrant for the deterministic extrapolation to the conclusion that all mental events are the necessary consequents of preceding causes. This feeling, perhaps not misdescribed as such, has greatly contributed to what has long been a philosophical familiarity, an attempt to have both of freedom and determinism. The strategy of many philosophers has been to accept that choices and decisions are or may be caused, and to argue that, none the less, we may be confident of our freedom. Their position, which I shall now consider, is that determinism is compatible with our ordinary beliefs to the effect that we sometimes choose and decide freely.

3. The Compatibility Theory

The problem of human freedom, we are persistently reminded, has long since been solved. Indeed, we have been told, it is 'really one of the greatest scandals of philosophy that again and again so much paper and printer's ink is devoted to this matter. . . .'[6] The supposed solution was stated by Hobbes and has since Hume been a traditional part of what may be called the empiricist conception of man.[7] The problem is the seeming incompatibility of the belief that such things as decisions are caused and the belief that sometimes we decide freely. The solution of those who hold what we may call the compatibility theory is that these two beliefs, contrary to what is supposed,

6. Moritz Schlick, *Problems of Ethics* (New York, 1939), translated by David Rynin, p. 143.
7. See, in addition to Schlick, *op. cit.*, and the works mentioned below: A. J. Ayer, 'Freedom and Necessity', *Philosophical Essays* (London, 1954); C. L. Stevenson, *Ethics and Language* (New Haven, 1944), Chapter Fourteen; Philippa Foot, 'Freewill as Involving Determinism', *Philosophical Review*, 1957; Paul Edwards, 'Hard and Soft Determinism', in *Determinism and Freedom* (New York, 1958), edited by Sidney Hook; John Hospers, 'What Means This Freedom?', in Hook, *op. cit.* The, or one, genesis of the doctrine is to be found in Aristotle, *Nicomachean Ethics*, Book Three.

are perfectly consistent. To see this we need only get clear about the correct meaning of the word 'free' and related words. The word 'free' is taken, by those who hold the compatibility theory, to mean something like 'unconstrained' or 'uncompelled', and it is claimed without fear of denial that there is no incompatibility between the claim that all decisions are the necessary consequents of preceding causes and the claim that in general we are not constrained or compelled to decide as we do. It in no way follows from the fact that my decision was caused, for example, that I did not want to make it.

It requires but little ingenuity, of course, to find a conception of freedom such that freedom and determinism are consistent. If to decide freely is defined as opting for something in the belief that some doctrine of determinism is true, then deciding freely and determinism are in no way opposed. Again, some of us may be both determined and free if free decisions are those made by men who live by the instincts of war, are indifferent to travail, and in other ways satisfy Nietzsche's requirements. The arguments advanced for the compatibility theory, which certainly is to be distinguished from these curiosities, are not arguments to the effect that decisions may be both caused and unconstrained. This may be assumed. Rather, they are arguments which purport to show that the particular meaning given to 'free' and many related words is the one *relevant* to the dispute about human freedom.

Originally, within the tradition of thought we are considering, a man was said to be free when he was not kept from doing as he pleased by a physical force external to him.[8] The paradigmatic case of a lack of freedom was taken to be a man in fetters or in jail. This conception has the consequence, paradoxical at least to us, that a man who acts under threat is perfectly free in his action. On a revised view, to say that we sometimes act freely is to say that we have 'a power of acting or not acting according to the determinations of the will; that is, if we choose to remain at rest, we may; if we choose to move, we also may'.[9]

8. Hobbes, 'Of Liberty and Necessity', *English Works*, Volume Four.
9. Hume, An *Enquiry Concerning Human Understanding* (Selby-Bigge edition), p. 95.

H

This conception too has its obvious disadvantage, at least to us. Hume, its author, says rightly at one point that 'it is commonly allowed that madmen have no liberty', and yet, according to the account, it would seem that at least some have. Certainly they may possess a power of acting as they will. Finally, consider a more recent version.

> Freedom means the opposite of compulsion; a man is *free* if he does not act under *compulsion*, and he is compelled or unfree when he is hindered from without in the realisation of his natural desires. Hence he is unfree when he is locked up, or chained, or when someone forces him at the point of a gun to do what otherwise he would not do. This is quite clear, and everyone will admit that the everyday or legal notion of the lack of freedom is thus correctly interpreted, and that a man will be considered quite free and responsible if no such external compulsion is exerted upon him. There are certain cases which lie between these clearly described ones, as say, when someone acts under the influence of alcohol or a narcotic. In such cases we consider the man to be more or less unfree, and hold him less accountable, because we rightly view the influence of the drug as 'external', even though it is found within the body; it prevents him from taking decisions in the manner peculiar to his nature. . . . In the case also of a person who is mentally ill we do not consider him free with respect to those acts in which the disease expresses itself, because we view the illness as a disturbing factor which hinders the normal functioning of his natural tendencies. We make not him but his disease responsible.[10]

To say a man decided freely, then, is to say he was not constrained or compelled in his decision. That in turn means that *he decided as he wanted, unhindered by external or internal forces, and that he decided in a manner peculiar to his nature*. It seems evident that one may make such a decision even if determinism is true, even if all decisions are necessary consequents of antecedents. There

10. Schlick, *op. cit.*, pp. 150–1.

are many ways in which this analysis might be improved
without fundamentally changing its character. Were I going
to suggest that decisions which we ordinarily take to be
free do not fall under some such characterisation, rather more
precision would be desirable. My different claim will be that
while all of what we take to be free decisions are indeed unconstrained in something like the suggested sense, we do not take
them to be only this. Nothing but a radical addition to such
a characterisation, one which moves quite away from its
central idea, would make it adequate.

This would, of course, be disputed by a supporter of the
compatibility theory. The main argument advanced on behalf
of the theory, as in the quoted passage, is that its conception of
freedom is *the relevant because the ordinary* one. All we need do
is reflect on what people have in mind in their talk of free
decisions. We will see it to be nothing other than an absence of
compulsion or constraint. Imagine, we may be told, a trial
before a jury. The jurors come to believe on the basis of
evidence presented that the defendant was robbed of money
owned by his employer. An assailant threatened and knocked
him down in the street. The jurors believe that the defendant's
subsequent action in giving up the money was anything but a
free one. Surely, we are exhorted, it is obvious that their belief
is simply that he was compelled to do as he did. What else
is or could be in question? Suppose now that the jury, on the
basis of further and different evidence, comes to believe that
there was collusion between defendant and seeming assailant,
that the gun wasn't loaded, and that the defendant did not act
in fear. Clearly enough, the jury now regard the action of
giving up the money as a free one. It is clear, we are told, that
their belief is simply that the defendant was not compelled to
do as he did. What else could be in question?

That there is something else in question, if rarely in the
forefront of reflection, can be brought out quite easily. Let us
add the more extraordinary supposition that the jurors are
convinced, by a third presentation of evidence, that each of
the defendant's decisions relevant to the offence was the
necessary consequent of preceding causes. None of his decisions

could have been otherwise than it was, given the circumstance that obtained. No decision was constrained but none could have been different. If the jurors believe this, certainly, they again regard the action as an unfree one. We ordinarily do intend to convey, when we assert that a man decided freely, that he was not constrained, but this intention is to be understood against the background assumption that decisions are normally *not* causally necessary consequents. We take this as given. If we were to accept that a decision *was* such a consequent, then, whether or not constrained, we would not regard it as free. Assertions of free decision thus involve, normally, something explicit and something implicit. What is explicit is that someone was not constrained; what is implicit is that his or her decision was not a causally necessary consequent. It is false to suppose, then, that the compatibilist conception of a free decision is the whole of our ordinary conception.

This reply seems to me adequate, if too much on the level of the initial argument. Both argument and reply too readily assume that there is some single ordinary sense of 'free' and the many other terms in question. What seems indisputable is that there is *an* ordinary use of the terms, perhaps the most ordinary use, which is as I have described it. That it is an ordinary and perhaps the central use, however, is not sufficient to establish that it is that one relevant to the present discussion. This is another assumption of the argument which requires qualification. Relevance is dictated by particular concerns and interests, and what is relevant for one party to a dispute may not be so for another. We can give up the supposition that there is but one test of relevance. Most people who reflect on human freedom are concerned above all with what may be called, if opaquely, a question of responsibility. They are given to an extremely common conception of persons as agents and originators rather than causal phases, a conception sufficiently fundamental as to make full analysis difficult. For people who have this concern, the question at issue is *whether we are free in such a sense as to be responsible*. It happens to be the case, predictably, that this question makes use of an ordinary sense of the word 'free'. That it does so is not important. The conception at which I have gestured is one that has often been misconceived, usually in the interest of argument. To wish to know if we are responsible is not to wish to know if we may profitably be punished, blamed, rewarded, praised, or treated in related ways. At any rate, the questions can usefully be distinguished. It is simply false that the question of a man's personal responsibility, as usually conceived, is the question of whether punishing him, or whatever, will have good effects.[11] It is, in good part, a question of whether or not he could have acted otherwise than he did. I shall consider this element more closely in a moment. For the present, what I wish to suggest is that if we are asked to reflect on what people ordinarily have in mind with respect to questions and judgements of freedom, the best answer is that they are concerned with a freedom which involves responsibility. This would be true of our imagined jurors. What they have in mind, then, cannot be presented as merely a matter of constraint or its absence.

A second and now predictable argument for the compatibility theory is of a similar character. When we ordinarily speak of actions as free or unfree, it is said, our judgements have certain implications. If we say of a man's action that it was free, we imply that he may be treated in certain ways. If his action is taken to have been unfree, we imply that he may not be treated in these ways. Precisely such implications are had by the assertion that a man's action was unconstrained. This is indirect evidence that in our ordinary usage a free action is an unconstrained one and an unfree action a constrained one. The implication of a judgement that Green's action was a free one is that he may be praised, rewarded, blamed, or punished for it. The implication of a judgement that it was not free is that he cannot with justification be treated in any of these ways. There are the same implications with respect to judgements of absence of constraint and judgements of constraint.[12]

For reasons already suggested let us recast this argument. The concern of some people with human freedom, we may say,

11. Schlick, *loc. cit.* For the best known detailed reply see C. A. Campbell, 'Is Freewill a Pseudo-Problem?', *Mind*, 1951.

12. Cf. R. M. Hare, *Freedom and Reason* (Oxford, 1963), Chapter Four.

is rooted in a concern about the justification of such responses and practices as blame, punishment, praise, and reward. They wish to know if we are free in such a way that these things are in place. The given answer is that these things are indeed in place with respect to actions that are unconstrained. Since absence of constraint is consistent with determinism, they may put their worries aside. This answer requires, of course, that we accept a particular justification for punishment and the rest. It requires that we accept that punishment's justification does not presuppose any freedom on the part of offenders other than absence of constraint. For those who think otherwise, that the justification of punishment is wholly or partly retributivist, the fact that men's actions are often free in the sense of being unconstrained will not be of importance.

There is a third argument, closely related to the first one, for the claim that the freedom compatible with determinism is the relevant one. Reformulated, it runs as follows. There are those who are concerned with the question of whether actions are free in such a sense that they could have been otherwise than they were. Their concern is with whether we can ever act otherwise than we do. They too can be reassured. The conception of free action as unconstrained *is* a conception of action that could have been otherwise. This argument depends on a particular analysis of what it means to say that something could have been otherwise than it was. The statement that a man could have acted otherwise than he did, it is claimed, means simply that he *would* have acted otherwise *if* he had so decided. To say that man could have decided otherwise than he did is to say that he would have decided differently if sometime earlier he had made a different decision than he did. To say Brown could have decided not to malign his brother today, when he did so, is to say that he would not have done so if he had made some decision earlier—if, perhaps, he had decided years ago to stick to the strict truth in such matters.

Given this view of 'could have' statements, obviously, they may be connected with statements about absence of constraint. If my action was unconstrained, although the necessary consequent of antecedents, it could have been otherwise in the given sense. Those who wish to know if we have a freedom to act or decide otherwise, then, need not think that determinism makes it impossible. The rejoinder to this argument, clearly, is that the recipients will reject the given analysis of their interest. They do not want to know if we are free in some sense such that we could act otherwise than we do, *in a particular and peculiar sense of the latter words*. They do not want to know if we *would* act otherwise *if* things had previously been other than they were. No doubt they believe this to be true. We do on occasion use 'could have' in the conditional way suggested by the argument, although perhaps not in conjunction with 'acted' or 'decided'. However, we also have a non-conditional use of 'could have' where to say that a man could have done otherwise means simply that he was then in a position to do it.[13] He did not in fact do whatever it was, as we imply, but he might have done it given things just as they were. He might have done it, given his past as it was. To come to the final point, it is *this* sense of 'could have' which occurs in the intended question about freedom. We wish to know if we are free in such a sense that we could act in ways other than we do, *in the sense of the latter words just indicated*. It is not true that the conception of a free action as an unconstrained but determined one is a conception of an action that could have been otherwise in this sense. There is no reason for thinking that free actions, in this sense, remain possible if determinism is true.

There is one more argument advanced by those who hold the compatibility theory. Hobbes, Hume, and most of their successors have been at pains to maintain that no coherent or satisfactory account can be given of our decisions and choices if they are *not* presented as the necessary consequents of antecedent causes. Briskly put, the claim is that interpretations of such terms as 'free decision', if not deterministic, are incoherent or unclear to the point of uselessness. It has usually been maintained simply, that if decisions are not causally related to antecedents they must be random events. But, it is said, this makes for an

13. The compatibilist analysis of 'could have done otherwise' is advanced by G. E. Moore, *Ethics* (London, 1912), Chapter Six. The criticism is due to J. L. Austin, 'Ifs and Cans', *Philosophical Papers* (Oxford, 1961).

absurd conception of decisions. If they were this, no man could ever be in any sense responsible for his conduct. Quite as obviously, it is said, it is simply false that decisions are of a random character, that they bear no relation to their makers' characters, personalities, desires, motives, perceptions, and so on.

'Random', by implication at least, is here used ambiguously. It may mean either 'not caused', which perhaps is its correct sense, or it may mean something like 'unrelated in any significant way to antecedents'. It must be granted, obviously, that any account of free choices which makes them random events in the second sense is nonsense. No such account, one hopes, has ever been offered. Can it be that any account of choice incompatible with determinism must reduce to some such thing? It has sometimes seemed that those who hold the compatibility theory have half supposed in this connection that a truth of logic supports their case. However, while it is necessarily true that decisions are either caused or random, where 'random' means 'uncaused', it is not at all necessary that if they are uncaused they stand in no significant relation to antecedents. That is, it does not follow from the fact, if it is one, that decisions are not caused, that they are in no significant way related to antecedents. Indeed, if decisions are *either* caused or quite unrelated to antecedents, we are all of us given to a mistake. We do not ordinarily think, and we do not act as if we think, that decisions are caused, that for causal reasons they cannot be other than they are. But neither do we think that they have nothing to do with perceptions, feelings, and personal dispositions. On the contrary, we think there are intimate connections. It must be admitted, certainly, that no adequate account of these connections has ever been given, which is to say that no adequate analysis of decision has ever been given. There have been metaphors and attempts of many kinds to give explanations of decision in terms of its supposed machinery. There are the notions of the Will and the Self, neither of them enlightening.

It seems to me that there is no reason here for abandoning the question of whether free decisions as ordinarily conceived are a reality. We need not turn to the doubtful reassurance of the compatibility theory. It is not as if we must choose either to describe free decisions in the compatibilist way or to talk nonsense. We do, and it is no surprise, have a working idea of free decisions. They are those which were unconstrained and which, in the unconditional sense, could have been otherwise. We may explain that to say they could have been otherwise is to say that they were not causally necessary consequents. We may add that they were related in significant ways to their makers' perceptions, dispositions, and so on. This description, in so far as it goes beyond the notion of absence of constraint, is alarmingly negative and vague. It is none the less intelligible. It is worth remembering, of course, that the alternative account of decision, which makes it a matter of causal sequence, goes no way at all toward explaining what must still be regarded as its unique character. Decision, supposing it to be causal sequence, is very unlike other causal sequences. As much is here left unclear or unsaid.

4. *Other Reconciliations*

The compatibility theory, while still with us in its original form, has for a time been paid rather less attention than certain related contentions. One of these is advanced as a denial of mechanism, that kind of determinism which involves a rejection of consciousness and so regards men as machines. Mechanism, it is said, is a matter of physical events and states and so has no relevance to what is quite different, human choice and action. It is no more than a bogy.

The fear that theoretically minded persons have felt lest everything should turn out to be explicable by mechanical laws is a baseless fear. And it is baseless not because the contingency which they dread happens not to be impending, but because it makes no sense to speak of such a contingency. Physicists may one day have found the answer to all physical questions, but not all questions are physical questions.[14]

14. Gilbert Ryle, *The Concept of Mind* (London, 1949), p. 76.

Moves in a game of chess are governed both by the rules of the game and in quite another sense by the players: by their choices, deliberations, intentions, intelligence, stupidity, and so on. The writing of good prose is governed both by rules of grammar and an awareness of style. There is no possibility of reducing the choices and deliberations of the chess players to the rules of chess. They are not this sort of thing. There is no possibility of reducing considerations of style to the rules of grammar. They are not that sort of thing. Questions about chess moves in terms of rules must not be confused with questions about them in terms of the players. Questions about prose with respect to grammar must not be confused with questions about prose with respect to style. It may be true that human behaviour, in some wide sense of that term, is governed both by physical laws and, on the other hand, by choice, intelligence, purpose, and the like. There is no contradiction or inconsistency in supposing this, and there is no question of supposing that truths about choice, intelligence, and so on may be reduced to truths about physical laws. Two kinds of question may be asked, not only one.

Taken literally this is an argument specifically aimed at mechanism. What we are told is that one thing, an action for example, may be 'in accordance with two principles of completely different types and such that neither is "reducible" to the other'.[15] An action may be 'explained' by causal laws which make no mention of consciousness. It remains consistent to explain it also by such notions as choice and intelligence. I have no wish to discuss mechanism or materialism, which is quite separable from our thesis of determinism. The claims put forward may also be taken in a wider way, such that they refer to determinism as we have conceived it. So taken, they are that such things as human actions may be subject to causal laws and yet free or responsible. Two kinds of question may be asked about them, and that they are caused does not exclude their being free and responsible. This is of the nature of Johnsonian declaration rather than argument. *Why* is there no inconsistency in saying of a man that his signing of a petition was both a

15. *Op. cit.*, p. 78.

matter of causal laws and also a matter of free choice or judgement in an ordinary sense? This must be true, of course, if there truly are separate questions about human behaviour, such that an answer to one has no bearing on answers to the other. It is not enough to turn to the compatible but irreducibly dual governance of chess moves and the writing of good prose. *If* there is no inconsistency in saying of the man that his signing was a matter of causation and also a matter of free choice, *then* his signing is in a way analogous to a move in chess and the writing of good prose. But what ground do we have for thinking that there is no inconsistency? The traditional compatibility theory supplies a particular analysis of free choice at this point. Certainly something is required.

(We may notice in passing that it is sometimes thought that since human choices, decisions, and actions are not merely physical events they cannot be explained by events and states that are entirely physical in nature. There seems no reason to suppose this. Certainly determinism as we have conceived it cannot be a purely physical theory.[16] It takes in both physical and mental events and states. In this, it is hardly unique. We commonly make particular causal judgements where the cause is physical and the effect of a non-physical nature. A determinism which involved a thorough-going materialism would be simpler, in the sense of containing terms of only one category. The determinism we have been discussing is in the related sense complex, but this in itself cannot be a serious objection. If we can in fact distinguish the terms of the causal relation, that they are of different categories is not an obstacle.)

A related view appears to turn on a distinction between an action and a motion. It is a mistake, we are told, to regard the physical or physiological causes of bodily movements as also the causes of actions.

No doubt a comprehension of the details of the bodily mechanism will enable us to provide a causal explanation of the fact that arms and legs get moved in such-and-such

16. Cf. Bernard Williams, 'Postscript', in *Freedom and the Will* (London, 1963), edited by D. F. Pears, p.141.

ways given such-and-such excitations of the sense organs. No doubt, too, a being who lacks the developed bodily mechanism with which intelligent human beings are endowed is incapable of performing various actions including the action of raising one's arm at will. But if we distinguish, as we must, between the rising of one's arm and the action of raising one's arm, it is not at all clear that if we offer a causal explanation of the former in terms of events within the bodily mechanism we are *eo ipso* offering a causal explanation of the latter.[17]

We are told, indeed, that 'absolutely nothing about any matter of human conduct follows logically from any account of the physiological conditions of bodily movement'. These propositions are asserted, it appears, on the odd assumption that determinism is the contention that neuro-physiological events cause movements of the body and limbs *and that therefore* actions are caused. If we suppose this, we face the difficulty that there is not a one-to-one correlation between bodily movements, however defined, and actions. When a man's arm goes up, he may be signalling a turn, or waving to a friend, or bidding at an auction. One sees which from the context. Equally a man can perform the action of warning somebody by gesturing, writing a note, speaking, or merely glancing in some direction.

Even given this eccentric depiction of determinism, the argument cannot establish the desired conclusion. It cannot establish the proposition that even if body and limb movements are the consequents of antecedent causes, this has no importance whatever for actions. It cannot establish this because there *are* logical connections between statements describing bodily movements and statements about actions. If both my hands are rising above my head during a certain time it follows logically that I am not digging my garden. In fact, a moment's reflection indicates that *any* sequence of bodily movements is inconsistent with very considerable numbers of actions. If all my bodily movements are caused, then

17. A. I. Melden, *Free Action* (London, 1961), p. 72. See also R. S. Peters, *The Concept of Motivation* (London, 1958).

my freedom of action is very severely restricted indeed. As I
have implied, however, there is a more fundamental objection.
   Determinism may without logical fault be the thesis that
physical events and states cause such things as decisions and
actions. There is no need to suppose that it must be the
indirect thesis that neuro-physiological events and states cause
large-scale bodily movements and that these in turn are
connected in some way with actions. Why should we think that
physical events and states cannot be regarded as the causes of
actions? It is a fact that while we are perfectly able to use the
notion of an action, we are not clear about its analysis.[18] Such
states of affairs are familiar enough. Are we to say, perhaps,
that actions are those movements of a person which are
purposive? Does this mean they are movements for which he
can give a reason, some reason or other? We do not have to
come to a decision on these questions and many like them for
our present purposes. We successfully discriminate between
actions and other things, notably mere motions. If we can do
this, we can consider whether actions are causally necessary
consequents. No reason has been given for thinking that we
cannot. We need not know everything of a class of events,
or arrive at a correct philosophical analysis of the covering
concept, in order to judge of them whether they are caused.
Indeed, if we had to do this, we should know very few causal
connections indeed.
   There is another attempt[19] to dissolve the problem of freedom
and determinism at which I should like to look more closely. It is
worth attention both as original and because it provides a
different view of some familiarities. Its stated object is more
adequately to defend the compatibility theory. If it is successful
it provides a new support for the theory.
   Most of our relationships with other people are said to

   18. The distinction between understanding and being able to give a
correct philosophical analysis of a term or proposition is perhaps due to
G. E. Moore, 'A Defence of Common Sense', *Philosophical Papers* (London,
1959). See especially p. 37.
   19. P. F. Strawson, 'Freedom and Resentment', *Proceedings of the British
Academy*, 1962.

consist in or to be governed by two different sorts of attitudes, *reactive* and *objective*. The first sort includes resentment, certain attitudes of love, gratitude, forgiveness. They are to a great extent dependent upon our beliefs about the attitudes of others toward us and reflect a kind of demand for goodwill or regard. They are at the root of a multitude of kinds of relationships, of which some are those between members of a family, colleagues, sharers of a common interest, friends, lovers, people who meet briefly in various situations of life. Consider now, for example, occasions when resentment is a possibility, occasions when we have been injured by someone's action or manifestation of attitude. We in fact do not feel resentment, or feel it less than we might, when we accept that the action was not intended or that the person could not help it. What is also true, on these occasions, is that we do not respond with a suspension of *all* our reactive attitudes. We do not respond by coming to regard the agent as an inappropriate object of such attitudes. On other occasions when resentment is a possibility, the injurious action may be explained (1) by pleas that the agent isn't himself or is under a great strain or, extraordinarily, that he is acting according to post-hypnotic suggestion. Alternatively the action may be explained (2) by pleas that he is only a child, or is schizophrenic, or subject to some known compulsion. On occasions of these kinds, of which the second group is more important, our resentment again is modified or disappears. Also, we are told, our *other* reactive attitudes to the agent are suspended or changed for a time or thereafter. When we see someone as warped or deranged, gravely neurotic or a child, *all* our reactive attitudes tend to be profoundly modified or to disappear. We move away from involvement or participation in a human relationship and toward an *objective* attitude.

To adopt the objective attitude to another human being is to see him, perhaps, as an object of social policy; as a subject for what, in a wide range of senses, might be called treatment; as something certainly to be taken account, perhaps precautionary account, of; to be managed or handled or cured or trained; perhaps simply to be avoided. . . . The objective attitude may be emotionally toned in many ways, but not in all ways: it may include repulsion or fear, it may include pity or even love, though not all kinds of love. But it cannot include the range of reactive feelings and attitudes which belong to involvement or participation with others in inter-personal human relationships; it cannot include resentment, gratitude, forgiveness, anger, or the sort of love which two adults can sometimes be said to feel reciprocally for each other.[20]

If we take up this attitude mainly to persons who are abnormal in something like the mentioned ways, or whose situations are abnormal, we can also adopt it with respect to those who are normal. We can retreat from ordinary reactive attitudes in order to avoid involvement with others, or for reasons of policy, or out of a kind of curiosity.

One of the questions to which these reflections are an introduction is this: Would our accepting that determinism is true lead to the decay of our reactive attitudes? Would it mean the end of gratitude and resentment, reciprocated adult loves, the essentially personal antagonisms? The answer given is that it would not, essentially for the following reason.

> The human commitment to participation in ordinary inter-personal relationships is . . . too thoroughgoing and deeply rooted for us to take seriously the thought that a general theoretical conviction might so change our world that, in it, there were no longer any such things as inter-personal relationships as we normally understand them; and being involved in inter-personal relationships . . . is being exposed to the range of reactive attitudes and feelings that is in question.[21]

A second question is this one: What would it be rational to do if we came to believe determinism to be true? That is, putting

20. *Op. cit.*, pp.194–5.
21. *Op. cit.*, p.197.

aside the question of what we in fact would do, would it be rational to attempt to retreat from reactive attitudes? This, it is said, could be 'a real question' only for someone who fails to understand the depth of our commitment to such attitudes. This commitment is integral to the framework of human life, not something that can come up for review. Furthermore:

> if we could imagine what we cannot have, viz. a choice in this matter, then we could choose rationally only in the light of an assessment of the gains and losses to human life, its enrichment or impoverishment; and the truth or falsity of a general thesis of determinism would not bear on the rationality of *this* choice.[22]

If we came to believe in determinism it would not be rational to be governed by what we took to be a true belief. If a belief in determinism were to lead us to suppose reactive attitudes out of place, in rationality we should persist in them.

Part of the argument, then, is that we would not and should not retreat from our normal human relationships if we came to accept determinism. The other part, so far unmentioned, is that when we *do* retreat in ordinary life it is not because we take the person in question to be somehow determined. We ordinarily move toward objectivity because we take the person to be abnormal, in some way incapacitated for ordinary relationships. Can we see this as a withdrawal because the person is 'determined' to act as he does? No. All that we could mean by the word is that he is abnormal or incapacitated. But, it is self-contradictory to suppose that everyone might be abnormal or incapacitated. The somewhat elusive point is this. When we *do* withdraw into objectivity, it is not for a kind of reason that could conceivably apply to everybody. Thus there is an obvious incoherence in saying that our reactive attitudes toward an individual change because 'determinism', something which necessarily might be true of everybody, is true of him.

In the remaining portion of this doctrine, the same conclusions are drawn with respect to certain *moral* attitudes, which

22. *Op. cit.*, p.199.

are presented as closely related to the reactive attitudes already described. Let us, before turning to this, examine what has already been said. The specific beliefs thought to lead to a shift toward objectivity in ordinary life are that the person in question is deranged or deluded, morally or intellectually undeveloped, neurotically compulsive in an extraordinary way, systematically perverted in some way. This account, as may be anticipated, seems to me crucially misleading. It is true, no doubt, that considerations of this kind almost always precipitate our withdrawals toward objectivity in the given sense. That these considerations are in the forefront of our experience, however, is so for the reason that we generally assume that something else is true. We assume that human choices and actions are not causally necessary, that individuals can choose and act in ways other than they do. If we believed otherwise of someone, this would as surely give rise to a departure from reactive attitudes. Consider resentment at a hurtful action.

We may cease to feel it if we believe the agent is schizophrenic or in some other way incapacitated. We would as readily come to cease to feel it, however, if we believed that he could not have acted in any other way than he did. The truth of this may be obscured in several ways. One may be inclined to doubt that resentment *would* disappear in the second case. Strong feelings, one may say, would persist. How, exactly, are they to be distinguished from resentment? But precisely the same difficulty arises in the first case. Given this, what may be put in question is the general distinction between reactive and objective attitudes, and any general claim about their genesis and persistence. We do not seem to have anything that suggests a distinction between our response to the given abnormal behaviour and what would be our response to behaviour believed to be determined. In the second case *as much as in the first*, surely, involvement and participation in a human situation would give way to taking account of the agent as someone to be handled, treated, or at least in certain ways avoided. Consider the reactive attitude of adult love. One may be inclined to say that we might not cease to feel love for someone whose behaviour was taken to be determined. It can at least be replied, though,

I

that our response would be similar if we came to believe the person to be in particular ways incapacitated or abnormal. Again, what is in question is the general doctrine about kinds of attitude and their persistence. What can reasonably be maintained is that a shift would take place as certainly if behaviour came to be regarded as determined as it would if the agent came to be regarded as incapacitated in one of the given ways. With respect to the reactive attitudes of gratitude and forgiveness, the contention can hardly be denied. These responses would not persist, certainly, in the face of a realisation that determinism was true of the person in question. We would feel that questions of forgiveness and gratitude did not arise.

Little needs to be said about the supposed incoherence of these claims. If one accepts of determinism that it might be true of everyone and also that to be subject to it is to be abnormal or incapacitated, there is a certain difficulty. Not all members of a group can be abnormal, certainly, by the test of norms derived from behaviour of the group. But there is no reason for accepting the conception of determinism as universal abnormality. The suggestion is that we must because (1) only beliefs as to abnormality could have the consequences in terms of attitude claimed by some for determinism and (2) no other intelligible account of determinism is available. Both propositions, for reasons already given, seem false.

To turn to the other contentions, would our acceptance of a general thesis of determinism lead to the decay of our reactive attitudes? The answer that it might do so seems as arguable as a denial. In this area, clearly enough, one can do no more than engage in entirely vulnerable speculation. It would be absurd to maintain that in some relatively brief space of time, as a consequence of some limited corpus of evidence, we might depart from reactive attitudes. The possibility of an evolution of outlook, as a consequence of constantly improving evidence, is another matter. This would not be the *end* of inter-personal relationships but their radical alteration. Would it be *rational* to attempt to retreat from reactive attitudes if we came to believe a general thesis of determinism? If we succeeded, it was implied, our existence would cease in some sense of the word to be human. Given this, if we had a choice, the rational course would not be to attempt to change our attitudes. As was rightly maintained, the question at issue is an entirely hypothetical one. Our attitudes might or might not change, but that they might change or persist as a consequence of *decision* is impossible. What is also true is that a continuation in reactive attitudes as we have conceived them would be inconsistent with our new view of persons. It would imply that they could choose and act in ways they could not.

All of this doctrine is an exercise in philosophical strategy. It is an attempt to get clearer about freedom and determinism by turning one's attention from a field where vision is obscured by doctrine to a neighbouring one. As we have seen (pp. 107–8), it has always been maintained by those who hold the compatibility theory that even if determinism is true, we can continue in certain of our moral responses. We can, for example, continue to regard punishment as justified. We cannot regard offenders as in a certain sense responsible for their actions, but this is not necessary. Punishment is wholly a matter of prevention, of securing certain effects. So with acts of blaming, and responses of other kinds. The doctrine we have been considering bears on these matters. We have turned to the subject of determinism and non-moral attitudes, reactive attitudes, in order to see more clearly what is true with respect to determinism and certain moral attitudes.

Reactive attitudes are those that can be had by a person only because of the actions or attitudes of others *toward him*. They have analogues which are attitudes which may be felt by a person on account of the actions of others *toward others*. These may seem to be seen as disinterested, vicarious, impersonal, or generalised, and are said to be moral attitudes. They are attitudes to agents, rather than judgements about the rightness or wrongness of actions, and they centrally involve regarding persons as in a way responsible. There are also attitudes of a third category. These are those that a person may have to himself because of his actions toward others. If we begin with resentment as an example of a reactive attitude in the original sense, its moral analogue in the second category is moral indignation or moral disapprobation. It is also related to the third-category feelings of being responsible, of shame, and of guilt.

Predictable claims are made. If a man acts toward another in a certain way we may feel moral indignation. If we come to believe, say, that he acted out of a certain kind of ignorance, our attitude changes. If we come to believe he is in certain ways abnormal, perhaps someone whose picture of the world is a complete delusion, it is again true that our moral indignation changes or disappears. More important, however, we tend to cease to regard him as a fitting object of *any* moral attitude. He is not seen 'as a morally responsible agent, as a term of moral relationships, as a member of the moral community'.[23] He is not someone of whom one can say in a certain way that he ought to have done this, was responsible for that, or deserves moral condemnation for something else. Would acceptance of some general thesis of determinism lead to the decay of these attitudes? Would it be rational to attempt to inhibit such attitudes if we came to believe such a thesis? Do we ever retreat from such attitudes with respect to a particular person, in ordinary life, for reasons of determinism? In each case the answer given is no. The reasons are exactly parallel to those given in connection with the attitudes discussed earlier and are open to the same rebuttals.

I said a moment ago that these reflections were intended to give a kind of support to the traditional compatibility theory. In order to defend that theory, its supporters conceive punishment and indeed ordinary moral judgements about individuals as no more than instruments of policy, treatment, or control. It is only by so conceiving them, it is supposed, that they remain a possibility in the face of determinism. In effect, supporters of the theory reconcile these things with determinism by assigning to them what we have been calling an *objective*-character. They make them the expressions of objective attitudes. If the argument we have been considering had been successful, we would have the satisfaction of also reconciling determinism with moral responses of a different character,

23. *Op. cit.*, p. 202.

those which involve imputations of responsibility. The argument is not successful and that conclusion cannot be drawn.

I have not introduced discussion of the account of attitudes to make only these points, however. In considering free will and determinism, one is likely to overstate the importance of moral implications of one kind and another. There is very nearly as much reason, I think, to consider the problem in the light of other than moral attitudes. We wish to know, surely, if we are free in such a sense that what have been called the reactive attitudes are in place. This is an important interest, and like other such interests dictates a criterion of relevance. We have the conclusions, given all the above argument, that it is mistaken to think that *if* determinism is true there are no logical consequences in terms of reactive attitudes. There *is* the consequence that they are out of place.

5. *Believing Determinism*

If determinism is true, to bring together all that has been said, we are not free in such a way that we are responsible agents, or can ever decide or act otherwise than we do, or can regard the non-moral attitudes that shape our lives as in place. Nor are we free in such a sense that we may consistently persist in certain moral responses. These consequences of determinism are in several ways related one to another, but I shall say no more about them. What I wish to suggest instead is that there is one more incompatibility, more fundamental than these. It is unusaul in that it itself may be thought to have a curious consequence with respect to determinism.

If determinism is true, then *judgement,* in a certain sense, is impossible. Determinism is inconsistent with our most rooted conception of judgement and so, I shall suggest, if determinism is taken to be true there is no possibility of confident belief. It follows, further, given that our claims to knowledge presuppose belief, that if determinism is taken to be true we cannot claim knowledge. In particular, we cannot persist in the belief that determinism is true. We cannot continue to claim that we know it to be true. Any attempt to prove it to be true, then, will be self-defeating. All that we can possibly do, if we choose to reflect on the matter, is to come to believe it false. It may be suggested at this point, mistakenly, that if we cannot claim knowledge of the truth of determinism, we might none the less persist in regarding it as probable or likely. The answer, of course, is that if determinism is claimed to be probably true, then that very claim to knowledge of a probability is put in question.

The argument consists fundamentally in the claims that inasmuch as judgement of a certain kind is inconsistent with determinism, so is the possibility of confident belief and claims to knowledge. In considering this, let us admit first that thinking is not inconsistent with determinism. One would not hesitate to say, at any rate, that a man might *have the thought that* something or other was the case even if the events of his thinking it were causally necessary consequents. We regard the having of thoughts as something passive, as it was once common to say, and perhaps for this reason we are not opposed to the idea that having thoughts may be something subject to causation. Is this an attitude of absolutely general scope? It seems so. It seems true of the having of thoughts which are close reports of sense experience and it seems equally true with regard to, say, idle reflections, thoughts that certain things are relevant evidence for something, thoughts that conclusions are logically necessary or inductively well established. This is also related to, or perhaps identical with, the point sometimes made in the assertion that 'belief is involuntary'. Against this, however, we must put some other facts. They concern what may be called notions of judgement: those of judging, assessing, inquiring, investigating, appraising evidence, and a great many others. To do any of these things is, to say no more, not merely to have thoughts.

Assuredly there are possible but not actual uses of these terms of judgement, with respect to persons, that do not have the consequence in which I am interested. Suppose we imagine that someone is reflecting on determinism and wondering if the Law of Causation is vacuous, thinking that it isn't, perhaps reflecting on the kinds of evidence for it. We might say of him that he is engaged in an inquiry in the same sense that we might say it of a computer. We might evaluate his procedure in a number of ways. Centrally, we might evaluate it as to the correctness or truth of particular beliefs to which he comes. One distinguishing feature of this situation we imagine, however, would be the absence on our part of a quite different evaluative attitude. As in the case of a computer, we would not in a certain familiar sense commend the thinker for his performance, give him credit for it. It would not be that we would give it to someone else, or something else, but rather that the question would not arise at all. What I have in mind will be clear, I think, if the main distinguishing feature of the imagined situation is made explicit. It is, simply, that we take it that each of the thinker's reflections is a causally necessary consequent. Whatever answer or speculation he comes to, or indeed whatever question, his coming to it is a matter of causal determination.

We might say of a thinker of whom we imagined this to be true that he was in a sense making judgements, testing hypotheses, considering propositions for consistency. Nevertheless, there is another use of such descriptions which we would take to be out of place. We certainly would not be surprised if someone said something like this: 'If what is true is that he couldn't at any moment think anything other than he does, given causal antecedents, it's absurd to say that he's really judging or carrying out an inquiry at all. He's not doing anything. All that's to be said is that things are happening to him.' It would not come as a surprise to be reminded that there is a use of descriptions of intellectual sequences that involves the assumption that they are not matters of causal necessity. Indeed, this may be said to be the central ordinary use of such descriptions.

What I wish to suggest is that if we could judge only in the first sense and not judge in this second sense, the ordinary one, we could not have confident belief and make claims to knowledge. It is a requisite of my coming to such beliefs that I take them to be the product of a kind of process which is impossible if determinism is true. It is easy here and elsewhere to succumb to one of the persistent temptations of this discussion. It is easy to assert that we take ourselves to know that something is so because the evidence *is* this or that and *does* support the conclusion. This is no more than a concealing abbreviation. The evidence does not announce the conclusion. It is nowhere near a sufficient condition for my claiming to know that I am here that in fact I am here. But, it may be said, something like this may be true without it being necessary that we regard our beliefs as products of judgement that is not causally necessitated. Let us consider some possible objections.

'Perhaps', someone suggests, 'you are reluctant to say that we could claim to know something under the supposed conditions because you are impressed or worried by what is essentially an irrelevant consideration. As you have implied, if we could be said to know anything under conditions of determinism we could not, in a certain sense, *take credit for it*. I suppose there is some sense of the words in which this is true. We could not take credit or be commended, because none of our beliefs would seem to be related to our doing. It could be said, if the language fits, that our beliefs happened to us. But none of this goes any way toward explaining why we couldn't have confident beliefs and claim knowledge if determinism was true.' This supposed explanation of error seems to me ineffective. People may find determinism, in so far as it has consequences for certain fundamental attitudes to themselves and others, a consequential doctrine indeed. It is, in a way, diminishing. It will be in place to consider such a diagnostic explanation of the claim that is being advanced only after the reason for it has been examined.

Alternatively, another attempt might be made to explain the supposed mistake. 'Perhaps what is bothering you,' it might be said, 'is that in ordinary life we do sometimes explain what we take to be errors by what seem to be causal explanations. Take the case where a man is called upon to judge the probable results of two possible courses of action. One of these is an orthodox course, the other a revolutionary one. He himself is a man of strikingly traditional and circumscribed outlook. We believe, when he finishes his investigation, that he has judged

the likely consequences of the two courses of action very
badly. We may say that he has done so because, given his
outlook, he is incapable of an impartial and generally perceptive
analysis of what is in question. It may seem, that is, that we
connect mistaken judgements with their being caused. Perhaps
this is what moves you to feel that determinism and confident
belief are incompatible. But, if you reflect a bit more, you will
see that just the kind of explanation given of the man we have
just imagined can be given of someone we take to have made a
perfectly correct estimate of something or other. In this case,
what we say is that he came to the right answers because he
is a man of certain character, one such that his inclinations do
not distort his judgement.' This supposed explanation of error
may be an explanation of the attitudes of some people. There
is no reason for supposing that the claim I intend must rest on
any such misconception. Nor do I accept, of course, any
implication of the objection that we *normally* take judgement
to be causally necessary.

Suppose now that we ourselves are asked to make some such investigation as the one just imagined. In the past we have carried
out such investigations and then been forced to the realisation
that we made mistakes. Someone now says, of our present
conclusions, that they seem to him mistaken. He does not show
how. He says only that our having made mistakes comes as no
surprise because he considers us incapable of surmounting the
effects of prejudice. If we are moved by this at all, I contend, it
will be impossible to avoid doubt about our conclusions.
What we may say or do, of course, is another matter. The
ground of the doubt will be that we are impressed by the claim
that we could not have decided otherwise than we did. It may be
objected at this point that we might indeed have doubts, but only
for the good inductive reasons of our already proven fallibility.
It may be replied that while there are such situations, it is also a
familiar fact that there are situations of just the sort suggested.
In any case, precisely the same argument can be made out with
respect to a man who has a splendid record of getting things
right. If I am him, and *if* somebody produces a convincing
argument to the effect that because of a cause inherent in

a certain situation I was incapable of concluding in any other way than I did, I shall fall into doubt. I shall take more convincing of the alleged incapability than in the previous situation, but that is not really important. What is important is my response *if* I do come to believe I could not have concluded in any other way.

A particular distinction is worth reiterating at this point. That what we take to be true *is* true is a matter of the way things are. That it *is* true or false is a matter of the facts as they are. In the usual case, the truth or falsity of what we believe does not depend on how we came to believe it. I may come to believe what is true by an absurdly irrelevant process of other way than I did, I shall fall into doubt. I shall take more reflection. I am not at present interested in the conditions of beliefs to be true. Under what conditions can we have confidence in what we believe? The examples indicate that a necessary condition of having confidence in a belief p is the further belief *that one could have come to some belief other than p.* That is, a necessary condition is that the belief was not a causally necessary consequent. It is no good saying that we have confidence in our beliefs when we think they reflect the way things are. Certainly it is a necessary condition of my believing something that I take my belief to correspond to the facts. There is a prior question, however. It is this one: Under what conditions can I be confident that my beliefs *do* correspond to the facts?

What is it that leads us, or leads some of us, to resist the claim that we might have confidence in a belief while thinking that we could not have come to any other? The explanation, I think, is that having confidence in a belief requires us to think that we have good reasons for it. We must think, that is, that the thoughts which produced the belief were in fact good reasons for it. Certainly they *might* have been just this. It is not that we believe they could not have been.[24] The difficulty is that *whether or not* they were good reasons for the belief, it necessarily was their consequent. Is there some confusion here? Is it open

24. As is suggested by A. J. Ayer, 'Fatalism', *The Concept of a Person and Other Essays* (London, 1963), p. 266.

to someone to say that we might have good reasons for the belief whether or not the thoughts which produced it were such? It is true, of course, that there might *be good reasons for the belief*, where that means simply that the belief may be true. What we are after, however, is something in consciousness that gives support to the belief, reasons in the sense of thoughts. Any of these, however, given determinism, give rise to beliefs as effects.[25] That they are, as we say, *good* reasons or *bad* reasons, is immaterial. Their causal properties, to put the matter one way, are not their logical properties. The belief that p may be an excellent reason for the belief that q and a reason against the belief that r. But why should we think that the first belief *causes* the second and does not cause the third?

It may seem, at this point, that what is demanded is that we *only* move from beliefs which are good reasons for certain propositions to beliefs in those propositions. That is, it may seem that the demand amounts to the requirement that we never fall into error. This is an absurd demand and, it may be said, it is similarly absurd to argue against determinism on the ground that it does not exclude the possibility of error. This is misunderstanding. What is being claimed is that if we are to stay confident in a belief we must believe we have good reasons for it. Its seeming correctness for us depends, as it must, on the thoughts we have had. If we accept determinism we must take it that these reflections would have produced the belief whether or not they were good reasons for it.

I have, I am afraid, already said about as much as I am able to bring into literalness and clarity in support of my contention. That confident belief requires judgement, in the ordinary sense, is to some people a very nearly irresistible claim. To some others, perhaps few in number, it is resistible. One's reaction presumably has to do with self-images that are out of clear view, in a way beyond adequate conceptualisation. It

---

25. That reasons, in this sense, can be causes seems to me true but should, no doubt, have been argued. See Alasdair MacIntyre, 'Determinism', *Mind*, 1957; Donald Davidson, 'Actions, Reasons and Causes', *Journal of Philosophy*, 1963; David Pears, 'Are Reasons for Actions Causes?', in *Epistemology* (New York, 1967), edited by Avrum Stroll.

is notoriously true that we lack enlightening or satisfying descriptions, of a positive nature, of judgement in the ordinary sense. We would like to have something specific and tangible about the supposed relationships between one's evidence-beliefs or premiss-beliefs and one's beliefs that certain conclusions are true. We should like to have useful concepts much less crude than those which have been pressed into service in this discussion. It does not help to declare that conclusions must be derived from active reflection. Nor is there help to be found in recourse to such phrases as 'the Faculty of Judgement', or in recourse to the elusive notion of rationality. There is also the embarrasment that one cannot give an effective explanation of why better descriptions of ordinary judgement are not forthcoming. All that one has is the feeling that there is some sense in the irritating utterance that thought cannot take itself as its object.

These are excellent reasons for a certain hesitancy of argument. They are not good reasons, it seems to me, for abandoning the point of view. The alternative conception of judgement, as something of which determinism is true, is as far from being a paradigm of completeness and clarity.

6. *Implications*

Determinism is not to be put aside as insufficiently intelligible to allow for useful discussion. The state of our understanding of the causal relationship does not give us this conclusion. Nor, although I have not paid them much attention, do certain difficulties in the philosophy of mind. These pertain, in the main, to determinism conceived as a doctrine of wholly mental causation. Determinism, secondly, is not to be reconciled with our notions of freedom in the traditional way of the empiricists. That there is a conflict is not to be evaded either by the familiar stratagem having to do with constraint or the several successors to that doctrine. If determinism is true, our conception of persons as responsible agents is false, we cannot decide or act otherwise than we do, and our reactive attitudes and some of our moral responses are not in place. Furthermore, as I have

just suggested, if determinism is true we cannot persist in
confident belief or advance claims to knowledge. At this point,
however, I wish to correct a certain impression.

There seems to me no point in refusing to recognise the
extent of the conflict between determinism and other things.
It is greater than many philosophers have supposed. At the
same time what has been said about belief and knowledge-
claims should not be misconstrued. It seems to me true that we
could never come to accept determinism in the way that we
now accept many things. We can never, with respect to determinism, have a part of what we now regard as necessary to
confident belief. It is not too much to say that we can never
have about it what we now describe as confident belief. This
is not to say that we can never come to *accept* it. If we were to
do this, our concepts both of belief and its grounds would
necessarily change. We would not have what we presently
count as beliefs and grounds. These changes in themselves,
putting aside other consequences of the acceptance of determinism, would amount to a transformation in outlook. That
it would be a deeply fundamental one is not a reason for thinking that it could not occur. It seems possible that there have
been others in the course of human development.

Through all this there persists the question of the truth of
determinism. A long discussion of the evidence, given the
evidence that seems to exist, would give rise only to an answer
that is already familiar. The issue is not in fact decidable.
I am inclined to add that this description of the state of affairs
is at least misleading. It seems true that there is a considerable
difference between the way in which we come to decide particular propositions about the world or ourselves and the way
in which we come to change more inclusive conceptions which
underlie and govern large areas of belief. It cannot be false or
misleading to say, however, that there remains a question
about human freedom and responsibility.

A justification of punishment wholly or partly in terms of
retribution, then, makes what must be regarded as an assumption. We may then add a question to the criticism already made
of traditional retributivism. The same question arises with

respect to those attempted justifications which are in part retributivist. A related question faces those critics of retributivism who begin from an assumption of the truth of determinism. It also faces those who regard criminality in a certain way as a consequence of some quite general doctrine of determinism. To anticipate what I shall suggest is the best defence of a practice of punishment, it does not require an assumption of freedom in the way of retributivist theories. That possible justification of punishment does not depend on the assumption that men can act otherwise than they do. Given our present attitudes the acceptance of that justification, like any other belief, does require that we are able to judge differently than we do.

5
Compromises

1. *Retrospect and Prospect*

THERE no longer are defenders of the traditional retribution theory, or at least of the version that we are obliged rather than permitted to punish offenders because they deserve it. At any rate, there are no defenders writing in the usual places. The causing of distress or suffering to offenders, mainly to give relatively small vindictive satisfactions to others, would no longer be regarded by any significant number of people as morally permissible, much less obligatory. The traditional deterrence view is also in decline,[1] for different reasons, if not so abandoned as the view that punishment is justified by reformative effects. On the other hand, the related belief that treatment rather than punishment would be justified by its effects alone is very much a part of the outlook of many people concerned in practical ways with criminality and other social problems. Whatever the popularity of these four views, it seems to me established that none of them is defensible.

What is also established, by the arguments from victimisation and indoctrination, is that no combination of reasons of deterrence and reform is sufficient to justify either punishment or a system under which some offenders are punished and others treated. One other objection to the traditional deterrence theory, or at any rate its application, it will be recalled, was that

---

1. There remain defenders of the related claim that punishment, when it rather than treatment is in place, is to be justified by its deterrent effect alone. See T. L. S. Sprigge, 'A Utilitarian Reply to Dr. McCloskey', *Inquiry*, 1965.

a considerable number of individuals are either unlikely to be influenced or quite certainly not to be influenced by the prospect of punishment. One obvious way of avoiding *this* objection is to recommend a selective system of punishment and treatment. If such a system were given over to only the aims of reducing offences and rehabilitating offenders it would face the objection about victimisation. Also, it might well involve unacceptable indoctrination. If it did not have possible consequences of victimisation, it could not be that it was governed only by the aims of prevention and rehabilitation.

Retributivism of the traditional kind mainly fails because it pays attention only to certain desires, or at least pays them too much attention. In effect, it ignores the welfare both of offenders and of those individuals who may be harmed by future offences. It has the recommendation, on the other hand, that since it treats offenders and others as they deserve, it prohibits unacceptable victimisations. The forward-looking theories, those of deterrence and reform, are quite given over to the pursuit of welfare. They fail, in the view of a number of contemporary philosophers who have considered them, because they ignore desert. Given this, it has seemed possible that a solution to the problem of punishment can be found in a compromise. Punishing a man is justified, it is supposed, if two conditions are satisfied. The punishment must be deserved and it must prevent offences in the future. What remains of traditional retributivism is but one part of the supposed obligation, that part which limits or prohibits punishment rather than demands it.[2] We are said never to be obliged to punish because it is deserved but rather to be obliged *not* to punish if it is not deserved.

I should like to look at some accounts of this kind although, of course, we have already anticipated some questions that will arise and settled others. In the first chapter we arrived at a certain account of the meaning of desert claims as used by retributivists. To say a man deserves a penalty may be to say (1) that he has behaved culpably, (2) that his penalty would satisfy a grievance caused by his action, (3) that his envisaged treatment

2. Chapter One, Section Three.

would be like the treatment of similar offenders, (4) that freely and responsibly he acted in such a way as to fall under a known penalty system, (5) and that unlike non-offenders he has gained satisfactions through the commission of an offence.

In the second chapter we saw that in certain circumstances which allow for choice, a punishment would be preferable to a victimisation.[3] This preference could be defended by elements of the argument that the punishment would be deserved. However, on further analysis, this defence was clarified as the proposition that the punishment would be more economical of distress than the victimisation. We also concluded earlier in the second chapter that in a certain circumstance doing nothing at all would be preferable to a possible very unfair victimisation.[4] Again, the preference could be defended by the claim that the victimisation would be undeserved. Here, however, this could be understood only as the proposition that the victimisation would make for gross inequality of treatment. Thus we came to regard desert claims as either appeals to equality or essentially utilitarian appeals for the minimisation of distress. The compromise theories of punishment attempt to justify it partly by the argument that it is deserved. It is not seen or granted, however, that this argument can be no more than an appeal to one or both of equality and economy. If it can be no more than this, these theories are unclear or confusedly claim a defence of punishment that does not exist. I shall amplify this in discussing them.

There is one related point to be noticed. I have said that to support a man's penalty as deserved is ordinarily to say, partly, that his action was free and responsible. This is inherent in the contained propositions that he behaved culpably and in contravention of a known penalty system. It is undeniable that this is a part of what is intended by the usual talk of desert. It is part of what is intended, certainly, in the arguments of the traditional retribution theory and all or almost all compromise theories. It would be mistaken, therefore, to suppose that human freedom is not a direct presupposition of these views.

3. Chapter Two, Section Five.
4. Chapter Two, Section Four.

K

We may, however, produce radical variants of them in which the argument from desert is specified as having only the force of an appeal to equality and economy. I shall consider such a compromise theory. Here, that a man acted freely and responsibly will *not* be a presupposition. Here the argument from desert, still reasonably so called, will be that punishment may be in accord with principles of equality and involve a lesser distress than victimisation. The latter part depends in part on the fact that offenders and possible victims have different expectations.[5] That they have these expectations does not depend on their having in fact acted freely and responsibly. That they have them depends on their having acted in accordance with, or in contravention of, the law.

2. *Logical Retributivism, Separate Questions*

Two things need to be cleared away before we come to consider several compromise theories. The first, which will have a certain familiarity, is a quite different 'reconciliation' of the traditional accounts of the justification of punishment.[6] Desert, we are told, is not a moral but rather a logical condition of punishment. That is, to say a man was punished although he did not deserve it, or, as it is usually expressed, was not guilty, is to say something self-contradictory. It is to say something self-contradictory in virtue of the meaning of the term 'punishment'.

. . . the necessity of not punishing the innocent is not moral but logical. It is not, as some retributivists think, that we *may* not punish the innocent and *ought* only to punish the guilty, but that we *cannot* punish the innocent and *must* only

5. Chapter Two, Section Five.
6. Anthony Quinton, 'On Punishment', *Analysis*, 1954; reprinted in Peter Laslett (editor), *Philosophy, Politics and Society*, First Series (Oxford 1963). John Rawls, 'Two Concepts of Rules', *Philosophical Review*, 1955. See also S. I. Benn, 'An Approach to the Problems of Punishment', *Philosophy*, 1958; Benn and R. S. Peters, *Social Principles and the Democratic State* (London, 1959), pp. 182–3; Arnold Kaufman, 'Anthony Quinton on Punishment', *Analysis*, 1959.

punish the guilty. Of course, the suffering or harm in which punishment consists can be and is inflicted on innocent people, but this is not punishment, it is judicial error or terrorism or, in Bradley's characteristically repellent phrase, 'social surgery'. The infliction of suffering on a person is only properly described as punishment if that person is guilty.[7]

To adopt the recommended definition of punishment, which does reproduce some ordinary understanding of the term, *is* to adopt the view that guilt or desert is a logically necessary condition of punishment. It is now argued, quite unconvincingly, that precisely this view has been the essential thesis of retributivism. It is claimed that retributivists have been merely concerned to assert that punishment can be of the guilty only, where this is an assertion not about what is morally allowable but rather about the meaning of the term 'punishment'. It will be evident that I take this to be false. Traditional retributivism is the doctrine that we are morally obliged or at least permitted to punish those who deserve penalties and prohibited from punishing anyone else. It is not the view that we are not to *describe* imprisonments or fines as punishment if those who are imprisoned or fined are not guilty. The compromise theories which we shall examine may be described as partly retributivist in that they involve some moral prohibition on punishing those who do not deserve penalties. They are not partly claims to the effect that we must, if we are to be self-consistent, describe as punishment only what is done to persons who are guilty of offences.

Of course, if one does use the term 'retributivism' for the logical or terminological claim, it will be possible to name diverse accounts of punishment as retributivist. One such account, if we make it explicit, is that punishments are morally justified if they deter economically and that only those impositions of distress that are deserved can correctly be called punishments. This is a formulation of the deterrence theory, with a morally irrelevant addition. We have already considered precisely this account, and also rejected the supposition that

7. Quinton, *op. cit.*, p. 86.

the addition is a barrier against victimisation-criticisms.[8] Defenders of this account, as we have seen, wish to maintain two things. (1) The given moral justification of punishment is in terms of economical deterrence alone. (2) Undeserved impositions of distress, victimisations, are not permissible even if they serve to deter economically. Either (1) or (2) must be given up. If the envisaged victimisations are not permissible, then it cannot be true that punishments are justified solely in virtue of being deterrents. If punishments *are* justified *solely* because they are deterrents, then certain victimisations would be similarly justified. There is one obvious line of retreat if it is thought that these victimisations would not be acceptable. One may take up some view of the kind we are about to examine. On the straightforward one already mentioned, punishments are said to be justified when they are both deserved and preventive of offences.

The second preliminary matter has to do with a way in which discussions of compromise views of punishment are commonly introduced. It will be worth looking at it briefly for several reasons. One is that it sometimes appears to be intended as something like an argument for the conclusion that punishment must be justified by several principles. Another is that it is regarded as a preferred or indeed essential mode of procedure. My own concern has been, and mostly will be, with the single question, 'What, if anything, can morally justify the practice of punishment?' A number of philosophers would regard this as an error, one with considerable consequences.

It has been said that in our inherited ways of talking about punishment we persistently over-simplify separate issues. What we must notice, if we are to avoid confusion, is that there is more than one question to be considered.[9] The institution

8. Chapter Two, Section Two.
9. H. L. A. Hart, 'Prolegomenon to the Principles of Punishment', *Proceedings of the Aristotelian Society*, 1959–60; Other separations of the questions are to be found in W. D. Ross, *The Right and the Good* (Oxford, 1930), p. 56; J. D. Mabbott, 'Punishment', *Mind*, 1939; P. H. Nowell-Smith, *Ethics* (London, 1954), p. 272; Anthony Flew, ' "The Justification of Punishment" ', *Philosophy*, 1954; Mabbott, 'Professor Flew on Punishment,' *Philosophy*, 1955; S. I. Benn and R. S. Peters, *Social Principles and the Demo-*

or practice of punishment has several features. Only certain persons are punished and only certain penalties are imposed. It therefore raises several quite separate questions of justification. There is the overall question, 'What justifies the general practice of punishment?' or 'What is the good of maintaining this institution?' This has been named the question of the General Justifying Aim of the institution. Secondly, there is the question of Liability. It is this: 'To whom may punishment be applied'? Finally, there is the question of Amount. 'How severely may we punish?' We are invited to see that there are these three distinct questions, and also to see that different answers are in place with respect to them. Surely the General Justifying Aim of punishment must be the prevention of crime. The answer to the question of who may be punished, surely, is that only those who deserve it or are guilty may be. A partly retributivist answer is in place, it may be urged, with respect to the third question. A man should not be given a larger penalty than he deserves. In some such way as this one is led toward the view that punishment is justified only by several different considerations. Let us consider this supposed persuasion of the truth of compromise theories before deciding on the supposed necessity of asking separate questions.

One is led toward a compromise view, we are told, by the fact that the first question is rightly answered in terms of prevention, the second rightly answered in terms of desert, and the third in terms of both. Whether these things are true, of course, depends on how each of the three questions is understood. As so far expressed, they are vague and ambiguous. Consider the second question, 'To whom may punishment be applied?' It is a long step in the direction of irrelevance to see this as peculiarly a question for a judge.[10] If one answers as if one were a judge, of course, there is a temptation to give the answer that punishment may be applied only to those who have

cratic State (London, 1959), Chapter Eight; Benn, 'An Approach to the Problems of Punishment', Philosophy, 1958; John Rawls, 'Two Concepts of Rules,' Philosophical Review, 1955; K. G. Armstrong, 'The Retributivist Hits Back', Mind, 1961.
    10. See Nowell-Smith, op. cit., and Rawls, op. cit.

broken the law. This may be to regard the question in a way which makes it irrelevant to the matter in hand. A judge may indeed be said to be justified in singling out for punishment those who have broken the law. This is to say, ordinarily, that his action is in accord with his powers and duties, as defined by law. But we are not inquiring into legality, into legal powers and obligations. We wish to know what can be said in moral justification of what is done by judges in accordance with their legal powers and obligations. Let us try to understand the given question, 'To whom may punishment be applied?', in another way, a way such that it might have the answer toward which we are being urged. It may be taken as this question: What if anything morally justifies our punishing only those who have broken the law? Could the fact that it is only these individuals who may be said to deserve punishment provide a *sufficient* answer to the question? Obviously not, since desert is not a sufficient justification for punishing any individual. This is plain retributivism, which has been rejected. It is rejected, indeed, by the philosophers whose compromise views we are considering. One might (skipping some other possibilities) take the question to be this: What justification is there for having as a feature of the practice of punishment some bar or prohibition against punishing those who are not offenders? As we have seen it is in general but not always true that we must not victimise, penalise non-offenders, if prevention is to be economical. This final version of the question, then, can be answered in terms of desert alone. We have a certain bar or prohibition because only offenders can be said to deserve penalties. This is to say, if my reductive argument about ordinary desert claims is correct, that we have the bar because it serves economy and equality.

One can give similar interpretations, with similar results, to the third question, 'How severely may we punish?' As for the first one, about the General Justifying Aim of punishment, it is ambiguous in a way peculiar to itself. It may be taken to be about the *aim* of punishment, which is certainly to be distinguished from its justification. It is sometimes true that to mention the aim of a particular line of action is to mention an accepted justification. On other occasions this is not so. My aim in badgering a man may be to get back a book he has borrowed; my justification may be that he promised to return it in a week without fail. It does seem true that the aim of punishment is prevention. The goal we want to achieve is a state of affairs where there are fewer offences committed. But it is clear that if the question about the practice or institution of punishment is to specify a part of our present inquiry, which is a moral one, it cannot be taken to be about only the aim or goal of the practice.

If we are asking what adequate moral justification can be given of the practice, it is quite mistaken to think that one can be given in terms of the prevention of offences alone. This is established by the argument about victimisation. Some such argument is accepted by those who espouse compromise theories. How then can they suppose that the moral justification of the practice can be prevention alone when they also require another different reason, in terms of desert? That this second reason may be related to a particular feature of the practice, the sentencing procedure, is immaterial. Something the same may be said, not that it matters much, for the reason having to do with prevention. One might mention the publicity of punishment. It is not at all clear, then, why anyone who feels that a compromise or two-value justification is necessary should also think the practice as a whole justified by only one of them. There is some explanation, no doubt, in the confusion of aim with justification. This confusion may be made easier, incidentally, by an assumption similar to one noticed above. That is, it is sometimes supposed that the question about the justification of the practice is peculiarly one for legislators. Legislators are concerned with a society's larger intentions, including the prevention of offences, although not exclusively so concerned. Even if they were concerned solely with aims, nothing would follow about the answer to our question. Of course one *can* formulate a moral question, in some sense about the practice, whose answer will be in terms of prevention alone. It is: What is to be said for the practice of punishment other than that it is governed in certain ways by rules of desert?

It seems that it is *possible*, then, to produce specific questions about punishment such that they may have different answers. These appear not to be the questions had in mind by the philosophers who have favoured this procedure. But that we can ask particular questions that *may* have the desired answers does not in itself establish anything about the answers. The mere fact that we can ask these particular questions is consistent with *all* the answers being solely in terms of prevention, or solely in terms of desert. There is no reason for thinking that some separate-questions procedure inevitably or logically leads one to a compromise theory.

Is it nevertheless true that one is likely to fall into confusion if one does not ask these questions, or some other set of separate questions? This seems to me mainly the claim that philosophers who have given single-reason answers about punishment, inadequate ones, would have done otherwise if they had asked separate questions. This is less than convincing. Utilitarians did not ignore the fact that there are prohibitions with respect to who can be punished and to what extent. In effect they isolated the question about the basis of these prohibitions and gave, as we have seen, partly mistaken answers. One can say of the traditional retributivists, similarly, that they were not unaware of the claim that the practice of punishment does have certain preventive effects. Following Kant, they commonly introduced this fact into discussion in order to deny its moral relevance.

Are *we* likely to fall into confusion if we do not ask separate questions? We shall not fall into the confusion of thinking that a single-reason answer to the moral question about punishment will do. Nor does it seem likely that we will risk other confusions. Certainly we must keep in mind the different features of the practice of punishment, and not only those having to do with certain prohibitions. We must consider what contribution may be made to the justification of the practice by particular features. But this we can do without a mechanical separation of questions.

Our fundamental and final concern, obviously, must be with the question of what justification can be given for the practice of punishment taken as a whole. It seems to me clear, although it is sometimes doubted, that this is a satisfactory formulation of the problem which *all* theories of punishment attempt to answer. This is not to say, of course, that all the answering theories have what might be called identical structures, although there is not much difference. Very briefly, retributivism rests on the nature of an offender's action and on only certain consequences of his punishment, the giving of satisfactions. (One might speculate about a kind of generalised satisfaction which derives from knowledge that the institution of punishment exists rather than from knowledge of particular instances of punishment.) The deterrence theory rests on supposed responses of individuals to their being punished and also on responses of others which derive from a knowledge of particular punishments and from knowledge of the existence of the institution. One of the traditional reformative theories of punishment rests on the supposed responses of both individuals who are punished and individuals who are not. Other reformative theories, those which advocate treatment, depend on supposed effects on the individuals treated. However, these theories too might include some form of the wider claim.

3. *Punishment and Rights*

So much for preliminaries. I should like now to look at the intricacies of four accounts of punishment which involve claims about both prevention and desert. They are expressions, in different ways, of persisting attitudes and errors. The first one is announced, quite mistakenly, as a view to the effect that while the justification of punishment is not to be found simply in terms of preventive effects, no part of it has to do with the desert of offenders. Rather, we are told, it is partly a matter of *rights*.[11]

The state is said to have a '*prima facie* obligation' to protect the rights of individuals, rights which may be infringed by criminal acts. It has a *prima facie* obligation to try in some way to prevent offences before they occur. However, there are certain principles which govern the measures it may take. All

11. Ross, *op. cit.*

individuals, including those accused of offences, start with rights to life, liberty, property and other things. These are rights against the state as well as against other individuals. In virtue of having these rights, each man has obligations to others. He has obligations to respect *their* rights. If he does respect them his own rights remain intact. If he does not, he loses them.

All of these propositions must be taken to be about moral rather than legal rights. It is not always true that a state is under any kind of moral obligation (even a *prima facie* one, the nature of which will be explained in a moment) to maintain legal rights. This is not the case if the rights in question lack moral justification, as many have. Given even that all of the legal rights of citizens *do* have a moral justification, they can give rise to the moral obligation in question only in virtue of their moral acceptability and not merely their legality. They can give rise to the moral obligation, that is, only in virtue of their status as *moral* rights. I do not wish to maintain, of course, that the existence of expectations which are founded on rights fixed in law does not give rise to *any* special moral obligations. What I wish to maintain and what is hardly controvertible is that there is no overriding moral obligation to maintain a *status quo* simply because it is supported by legal rights.

Suppose an offence has been committed. The state has a *prima facie* duty to try to prevent more offences of this kind, violations of the rights of individuals, and punishment may seem to be a means to this end. However, the state is under another *prima facie* obligation not itself to violate rights. Such *prima facie* obligations may be regarded as claims to which an action or practice may give rise. To be under such an obligation, it must be stressed, is not to be under an obligation in one ordinary sense. One can act in a way not in accord with a particular *prima facie* obligation and yet not be open to moral censure or reprobation. To be under conflicting *prima facie* obligations with respect to a particular situation is to be in a position such that there are reasons for and against a particular action. A consideration of *prima facie* obligations, however, at least in some cases, gives rise to an obligation in another sense,

COMPROMISES 145

an obligation whose breaking *does* involve moral blame. This we may call an absolute obligation. To return to the offence, consider the possibility of imprisoning Brown, who is *not* the offender. The state is under a *prima facie* obligation to Brown to respect his rights, and a *prima facie* obligation to all citizens to try to prevent the recurrence of offences of the kind in question. Unless circumstances are extremely unusual, such that society will be in extreme danger unless Brown is imprisoned, the emerging absolute obligation of the state is not to imprison him. On the other hand, consider the possibility of imprisoning Green, who *is* the offender. In this case the state is not under a *prima facie* obligation to respect his rights since he, in committing an offence, has not respected the rights of others. What is true here is that under certain conditions it is morally permissible for the state to imprison Green. It need not do so; it may if this is thought likely to prevent further offences.

We are told that this is not a justification of punishment in terms of prevention and desert. It is urged in this connection that it is not possible to assess an individual's culpability. In any case, 'for the state to make such an attempt would seriously interfere with its proper work. Its proper work is that of protecting rights'.[12] But why, exactly, on the given account, does Green lose his rights? Why does it become morally permissible to punish him but not Brown, assuming that the punishment will have a preventive effect? The reason given is that he has violated the rights of others. Clearly enough, though, if he had violated them in a completely accidental way, or involuntarily, it would not be thought permissible to punish him. One cannot but think, then, that the given reason is the claim that he deserves punishment. To say that he has violated a *right* is also to imply that his victim can make a certain claim. This is of secondary importance in the present context. What we appear to have is a partly retributivist justification of punishment. That this is mistakenly denied, or unseen, is partly to be explained in the following way.

Retributivism is characterised as the doctrine that we are justified in punishing for the reason that there should be a

12. *Op. cit.*, p. 60.

proportion between moral goodness and happiness. '. . . a state of affairs in which the good are happy and the bad unhappy is better than one in which the good are unhappy and the bad happy.'[13] But, it is said, it is impossible to assess the moral goodness or badness and the happiness or unhappiness of individuals. Judges would have to take into account their whole lives in order to do so, which is but one difficulty. What we actually do is different, and something which has a different justification. Legislators make certain actions offences and fix penalties for them. They are governed in this by the need to prevent such actions and also, with respect to the penalties, by the principle among others that 'the punishment should be proportional to the offence'.[14] A judge merely enforces the existing law, 'except when the law has allowed a scale of penalties within which he can choose'. In this case he chooses in accordance with the same kind of considerations that guide legislators.

To present these two accounts of procedure and justification in this way is slightly to disguise the feature that they share. In the second account, the legislators are governed by a principle of proportion, which cannot be other than a principle of desert. That this is done at a certain level of generality, not with respect to individual men and their acts, does not alter the fact. Judges also proceed partly on the basis of such a principle with respect to particular defendants. This is the standard case. It is not true, as the second account of the practice of punishment implies, that there is only a limited place for judicial choice between penalties. In short, there seems no good reason for denying that we here have a justification of punishment partly in terms of desert. It is, in effect, identical with the first account.

Is there anything to be gained by the terminology of rights? I think not. To say that the state has a *prima facie* obligation to protect the moral rights of citizens is to say that it has a *prima facie* obligation to prevent certain wrongful acts. Any further implications are not at present important. To talk of rights is to secure no significant advantage and to run the risk of mis-

13. *Op. cit.*, p. 58.
14. *Op. cit.*, p. 62.

takenly thinking that we are concerned merely with legality. Is there anything to be gained by the terminology of *prima facie* obligations? The answer again seems to be no. *Prima facie* obligations are moral reasons for action, claims to which situations give rise, and they are correctly and adequately described as such.

4. '*Because he broke the law*'

In contrast to the one we have considered, there are a number of doctrines advanced which pay attention to the need and value of preventing offences and yet claim to justify punishment solely on retributivist grounds. In one[15] of these we are told that our having laws and a legal system (if these can be separated) *is* partly justified by reasons of prevention. However, no part of the justification of punishing a man has to do with prevention. The justification, one that leads the author rightly to regard what he puts forward as other than 'orthodox' retributivism, is *simply that the man has broken the law*. His punishment, we are told, has nothing to do with desert. In this latter respect the view is rather like the one we have just considered. In its attempt to exclude considerations of prevention from the justification of punishment it is quite different.

Societies are said to be justified in having laws at all, rather than advice-systems or something of the sort, by the better effects. They are also justified in having particular laws rather than others partly by the effects.[16] The behaviour of citizens becomes to some considerable extent 'reliable and predictable';

15. J. D. Mabbott, 'Punishment', *Mind*, 1939; 'Professor Flew on Punishment', *Philosophy*, 1955. A lecture entitled 'Moral Rules' (*Proceedings of the British Academy*, 1953) is also of relevance.

16. This is the original claim, rightly described as a utilitarian one. In the later articles it is said that laws and rules are justified by the fact that *if* they were universally observed the effect would be better than if there were no such laws or rules. This is a departure from utilitarianism. Suppose it turns out that a particular rule is not universally observed and is unlikely to be. Suppose, what is more, that partial observance of the rule has on balance a bad effect. A utilitarian would give up the rule. This is not necessarily true of anyone who accepts that the rule is justified by the fact that *if* it were universally observed, the effects would be good.

the good citizen enjoys a certain security in his life. We may say for short that a part of the justification of law and a legal system is that it prevents certain kinds of behaviour. The other part has to do with the fact that the laws we have are such that offences and penalties are arranged in scales and the heaviest penalties are reserved for the most serious offences. It is explicitly said that this particular feature of the legal system is not to be explained, or not only to be explained, by the fact that because some offences are more harmful we are more anxious to prevent them and so provide heavier penalties.

There remains the independent question of what justifies the punishment of a particular man who breaks one of society's laws. '. . . one fact and one fact only can justify the punishment of this man, and that is a past fact, that he has committed a crime.'[17] For a number of reasons, which I shall consider in a moment, it is maintained that *no part of the justification* has to do with preventing offences. It is also maintained, for several reasons I shall consider, that the justification of punishing the man has nothing to do with the fact that he has performed an act of a certain desert.

> No punishment is morally retributive or reformative or deterrent. Any criminal punished for any one of these reasons is certainly unjustly punished. The only justification for punishing any man is that he has broken a law.[18]

What we have before us, then, amounts essentially to two propositions. The existence of law and the legal system is justified partly by utilitarian effects, partly by desert. Individual punishments, in contrast, are justified by rule-infractions. These propositions have their origins in a number of elisions and mistakes.

1. As is so often the case in such discussions, two questions which there *is* every reason to distinguish are run together. We begin as usual by asking: 'Under what circumstances is the punishment of some particular person justified?' The

17. 'Punishment', *op. cit.*, p. 152.
18. *Op. cit.*, p. 158.

answer, in effect, is that the circumstances are those in which a
person has broken the law, and in these circumstances a judge
is morally obliged to act. He is under a certain personal obligation since he has given an understanding. Perhaps there is
intended the further suggestion that he is under a legal obligation. However, it is clearly mistaken to think that an action is
morally justified simply because someone has promised to
perform it or is under a legal obligation to do so. The question
of justification has become confused with others. It is certainly
true that we cannot explain a judge's legal obligations by
pointing to preventive effects of his action in punishing an
offender. It is also true that we cannot explain a certain moral
claim upon him, deriving from a personal undertaking. This
goes no way toward showing that we cannot give a moral
justification of his action which refers to its effects.

2. There is also a related confusion. We begin with the
question of justification and then come to deal, as in the quoted
passage, with a quite different one: When is a punishment *just*?
There is all the difference in the world between these questions. A punishment may be just in the sense of being strictly
in accord with law or in the sense of being the deserved punishment. It may not be, in either case, that it is justified. The
traditional retributivist theory gives as the reason for punishment that it is just in the second sense. Our response to that
theory is that punishment's being just is not enough to justify
it. With respect to the present point, it is perfectly true that the
fact that a legal system has preventive effects does not make its
punishments just. They are just, to state one part of the requirement, only if those persons who are penalised have broken the
law. However, this is to go no way toward the desired conclusion that it is not possible that particular punishments are
justified by preventive effects.

3. We are told that preventive effects do not result from
particular punishments but rather from related things. Publicity
is given to punishments and it is through publicity that we
secure deterrence. Punishments are accompanied by reformative measures and it is through these that we may secure
reformation. In general, particular punishments cannot have

as part of their justification that they are preventive since they are not directly preventive themselves. To confine a reply to the question of deterrence, it simply is not true that the effect on the offender himself is not direct. Also, with respect to others, the contention ignores the unsurprising supposition that the public threat of punishment generally depends for its effectiveness on punishments actually being imposed.

4. Another argument may also be intended, one that is thought to have application to things other than punishment. It is taken to be established, for example, that the rule that one ought to keep one's promises is justified in a utilitarian way by its good effects. It is then maintained that there are occasions when keeping a promise will not have good effects and yet is the right thing to do. It then cannot be the case, we are told, that the justification of the particular action is to be found in its effects. The justification must be that the action is according to the rule that one ought to keep one's promises. In fact the justification of *any* particular action of promise-keeping is that it is according to the rule. This is, it is opaquely said, acting on principle. I do not wish to discuss these assertions in detail but simply to notice one thing. *If* one does accept that sometimes one ought to keep promises despite bad effects, one is not driven to the conclusion that the justification of any act of promise-keeping is merely that it is according to the rule. It is difficult to see, of course, how this is a justification at all in the relevant sense. One may rather conclude (1) that the rule is derived from, or based on, both a utilitarian principle of effects and also some other principle, and (2) that the same is true of individual acts of promise-keeping. A similar, and similarly failing, attempt may be made to maintain that the practice of punishment is justified in the main by its effects but particular impositions of punishment can be justified only by being in accordance with the rules that define the practice.

(5). Finally, with special reference to the submission that desert plays no part in the justification of particular impositions of punishment, it is maintained that no human individual has the 'status' to judge the immorality of another. That, one is to suppose, is God's business. We have already considered and dismissed the problems having to do with assessments of harm and responsibility. They have seemed to some to be insuperable problems, partly, because of the fact that standards for acceptable assessments have been set far too high.[19] Even if they were insuperable, and men's ways absolutely inscrutable to men, however, there would be nothing to be gained by recourse to the argument which is being urged upon us. It cannot be that the justification of any particular punishment is to be found in the fact, merely, that a man has broken the law. Facts of legality and illegality must be seen for what they are, no more. No one can maintain the rightness of punishments that have been imposed for offences against morally appalling laws. More important, it is clear that the bare fact that a law has been enacted making an admittedly wrongful act also an illegality is not the justification of the resulting punishments.

We must at least amend the proposition to this: the punishment of particular men is justified only by desert. Let us now consider this together with the other proposition, that law and the legal system are in part justified in a utilitarian way, by their effects. This conjunction is somewhat mystifying because of a problem about the logical relations of the notions of law and punishment.[20] We are at least willing to consider the idea that for there to be law, anything that would count as law, there must be punishment. We are ready to consider the possibility that to say there is a law is to say that there is punishment for a certain kind of behaviour. If we take up something like this account of law, then the pair of propositions we are considering becomes nonsensical, based on a supposed distinction that does not exist. We cannot have law justified partly by prevention and particular punishments justified wholly by desert. Things are not improved, however, if we take up an account of law which makes it logically independent of punishment. The doctrine is then that punishment is justified by desert and laws justified in the main by their effects. This leaves open the possibility that if the having of laws ceased to be justified by the effects, punishments would remain as justified as before. This is ordinary retributivism.

19. Chapter One, Section Five.
20. See Hart, *The Concept of Law* (Oxford, 1961).

L

5. A Right to Punish

One other recent theory announced as retributivist appears to be really two theories, one of which gives a large place to the preventive value of punishment.[21] It begins by distinguishing particular questions. There is the question of the definition of punishment, with which we are not at present concerned, and two others. (1) 'What, if anything, is the moral justification of punishment, with which we are not at present concerned, practice of punishment?' (2) What method or system of determining penalties is best? We are intended to take the first of these questions, despite its different expressions, as amounting to this: What moral justification is there for inflicting *some punishment or other* on people who break the law? That is, the question does not single out for inquiry any particular practice of punishment, one with a particular penalty-system. The second question *does* have to do with particular penalty-systems.

In answer to the first question we are told that we have some practice or other of punishment because we want to secure a number of ends or aims. We wish to protect society, reform criminals, deter others. These ends or purposes are 'morally and socially desirable' but they should not be confused with the moral justification of punishment. The moral justification of the practice is that it is deserved. (The argument given for this exclusion of the mentioned utilitarian values involves the confusion between just and justified punishment.) However, we are not *obliged* to punish because of desert. It is rather the case that because men deserve it we have a right to punish them. We vest this right in a judiciary. It is a right to punish up to a certain limit, up to what a man deserves for his offence. To what extent we exercise this right is a question that may be decided by reflection on the given aims of punishment. Given that we want to prevent offences and to reform men, it may sometimes be 'foolish or mean' to exercise the right.

Two things may be said about this. The first is that despite a certain ambivalence what has been said is plainly retributivist.

21. K. G. Armstrong, 'The Retributivist Hits Back', *Mind*, 1961.

We would, it seems, be justified in punishing even if there were no preventive effects. What else can be meant by the claim that we have the right to punish because men deserve it? As a consequence, this is as unacceptable as the retributivism considered in the first chapter. The other thing to be said about this answer to the first question is that it determines an answer to the second, the question concerning the justification of penalty-systems. We have not been given an argument for a practice of punishment of no particular penalty-system. Rather, we have been told we have a right to a practice such that men get penalties as severe as, but no more severe than, they deserve.

It seems then that the second question is already answered. It is answered again, however, and differently. A justified penalty-system is indeed one in which there are certain limits on penalties. No man is punished more than he deserves. However, we may be guided in the construction of such a system, and also in its application to particular men, by considerations of deterrence and reform.

> When the problem is to find the best system of penalty-fixing there is no doubt that a purely retributive theory would have serious weaknesses, both practically, because it may be very difficult to decide which of two crimes is the more serious and thus deserving of severer punishment, and morally, because if deterrent and reformatory considerations are altogether ignored when the list of penalties is drawn up a great social good might be sacrificed in order to achieve a small improvement in the accuracy of a punishment from the retributive standpoint. . . . a modified retributive theory is perfectly possible, one which only uses retributive considerations to fix some sort of upper limit to penalties and then looks to other factors to decide how much and what sort of pain shall be inflicted.[22]

It is suggested here that particular penalties are justified in virtue both of being deserved and being preventive. Some,

22. *Op. cit.*, p. 489.

although deserved, may *not* be justified. This is inconsistent with what has gone before. Also, it makes it impossible to regard the theory as retributivist. If one takes the quoted passage in the way that seems to be intended, and disregards what has gone before, what we have is clearly an attempt to justify punishment in terms of several principles.

6. *Explicit Compromise*

It should now be clear that any successful attempt at justification must give a real place both to considerations of prevention and, in some sense, desert. It is futile to try with one hand to let in prevention as part of the justification of punishment and with the other hand to exclude it. If it is let in, of course, there is nothing to be achieved but misdirection from describing the resulting view as essentially a retributivist one.

In my criticisms in the past three sections of this chapter, I have not touched on two essential points. One, mentioned at the beginning of the chapter, is that *any* compromise theory must include some attempt to explain the meaning and assess the force of arguments which mention desert. The theories discussed are also wanting in this respect. At least the last two of them, secondly, are wanting in that they are, or must be taken to be, claims that justified punishments are *always* both deserved and preventive. This is at least in question. In the second chapter above we noticed that there are already within the law many cases of what are regarded as justified victimisation.[23] Convictions under statutes of strict and vicarious liability may be such. Impositions of what I have called 'exemplary penalties' are also defended. Any adequate attempt to justify punishment, whatever its final conclusion, must deal with this question. It must consider the possibility that it is *not* always necessary to observe considerations of desert. (The question, incidentally, may be put in different ways. The definition of punishment we have mainly used does not require that punishments be deserved. One can then ask: Must

23. See above, p. 81 ff.

all justified punishments be deserved? One can require, of course, that anything that counts as punishment *be* deserved. We must then ask: Are *only* punishments justified?)

The most influential recent account of punishment[24] fulfils both these requirements: it at least attempts to explain the nature of desert-arguments; it does not assume that desert in some sense is a necessary condition of every justified punishment. Further, it is an account which makes no attempt to avoid the conclusion that punishment requires for its justification a recourse to arguments of different kinds. If it misdescribes this conclusion in a certain way, as we shall see, it is open to simple amendment.

The practice of punishment is said to involve a prohibition, perhaps justifiably overridden in certain cases, against penalising individuals who have not freely and responsibly performed an act which is an offence. This is explained and justified, firstly, by the consideration that they have responded in a particular way to a choice offered to them. The choice was between obeying the law and being left to themselves, or breaking the law and paying a price if found out. To defend the prohibition in this way, clearly, is to defend it by a part of our argument from desert.[25] Also, secondly, the prohibition secures that penalties are returns for harm done. In general, offenders have gained satisfactions in their offences; penalties are prices to be paid. This may seem a reiteration of the defence just given. I shall regard it as the claim that imposing penalties on offenders is a move toward equalisation of welfare and distress. So construed, this is again a part of our argument from desert. Punishment also involves a restriction, perhaps sometimes not observed for good reason, on the particular penalties that can be imposed. This is a feature explained and justified by a number of rules. (1) Penalties must not cause more distress than would occur if they were not imposed. (2) A penalty must

24. Given by Hart in a number of papers, all of them reprinted in *Punishment and Responsibility* (Oxford, 1968). In my account I have incorporated at least one of his later amendments to his original and best-known paper, 'Prolegomenon to the Principles of Punishment'.

25. P. 135, item (4).

not be imposed if a man's action falls under a rule of justification such as the rule having to do with injuring in self-defence. One of the aims of punishment is the protection of individuals from attack; it would be inconsistent, then, to punish a man for defending himself from attack. These two rules, clearly enough, explain and defend penalties by way of the principle of economical deterrence. The principle excludes judicial actions in opposition to the desired end of prevention and also requires that the end be secured only at a certain cost of distress. There are also other rules for penalties. (3) A man is to be excused a penalty if his act, although of a kind the law seeks to prevent, was unintentional, involuntary, or something of the sort. (4) He is to receive a mitigated penalty if he faced special difficulty in keeping the law, perhaps because of provocation. In both cases penalties are explained and defended by an element or our argument from desert. (5) Finally, a man is to be treated as others in his situation are treated. Similar offenders are to be similarly treated. This is also to explain and defend particular penalties by a part of our argument.

What remains to be said in brief exposition of the present doctrine is that it takes the practice of punishment *as a whole* to be justified *only* by its beneficial effect in preventing offences. I have already argued that it is impossible to maintain that the practice of punishment can be defended simply by reference to prevention. To attempt to do so is to attempt, in effect, to defend the traditional deterrence theory. Furthermore, it is inconsistent to maintain that the practice as a whole, taking into account all its features, does not have as part of its justification what is said on behalf of particular features. (Perhaps some ambiguity explains the fact that this claim is made. Can it be that when it is said that the practice or institution is justified only by its effects, what is oddly meant is that its *public* existence or character is justified only by the likely effects? Perhaps one could not justify this by an argument from desert. Such a point is not to be confused with a proposition about the justification of the practice as a whole.)

We can, of course, make an amendment to what has been said in order to exclude this misconception. Also, in order to preserve a certain continuity, we can state what has been put forward at the level of generality of the previous chapters. What I have in mind here is the rules of justification, excuse, and mitigation. To defend punishment partly by observing that it involves a rule of justification, as I have said, is to defend it by mentioning one way in which it pursues the prevention of certain actions as against others. This is implicit in the defence of the practice as an economical deterrent. To defend punishment partly by observing that it involves rules of excuse and mitigation is, as I said, to defend it by mentioning particular ways in which it is governed by considerations of desert. Deserved punishments, according to our analysis, have among other features this one: they are punishments of individuals who have, by actions for which they were responsible, contravened a known system of offences and penalties. Implicit in this are notions of degrees of responsibility, notions which may be summarised in terms of the rules of excuse and mitigation. The system itself may be regarded as incorporating these rules.

We lose nothing, given the purposes of the present discussion, if we describe the proposal before us in this way: A practice of punishment may in general be justified by the considerations that (1) it prevents offences economically, (2) those who are punished have performed actions for which they were responsible and which contravened a known system of offences and penalties, (3) similar offenders are treated in similar ways, and (4) imposing penalties on offenders is a way of equalising welfare and distress, since offenders have gained satisfactions through their offences. The words 'in general' have this importance: we are not given a final answer to the question of whether punishment may sometimes be justified even when those punished were not responsible for the offences in question. That is, we have not got a final answer to such questions as whether there is a justification for certain penalties imposed as a consequence of strict and vicarious liability.

I have already commented on the nature and force of the elements of such an argument for punishment. I should like once more to reopen the question and to take into account

certain suggestions as to its answer. What justificatory importance has the fact, taken by itself, than an offender has freely
and responsibly, at least to some degree, acted in a way
prohibited by a known system of offences and penalties? It is
not, we are told, that the fact is important because it entails
that the offender has behaved culpably. In every system of
criminal law 'there are necessarily many actions (quite apart
from the cases of "strict liability") that if voluntarily done are
criminally punishable, although our moral code may be either
silent as to their moral quality, or divided. Very many offences
are created by legislation designed to give effect to a particular
economic scheme (e.g. a state monopoly of road or rail trans-
port), the utility or moral character of which may be genuinely
in dispute.'[26] It may be true that not all offenders are morally
culpable but if this is so perhaps the systems of law in question
are partly unjustified. That is a possible reply. There is a better
reason for resisting the idea that the justificatory importance
of a free act against a penalty system is that such acts are
immoral. Even if this is so, why should this fact give us even
part of a licence to punish? As we have seen, it appears to be
impossible to extract anything like a moral reason for action
from the mere fact that a man has behaved in a culpable way.[27]
One may have a certain response which has its origins in
defensive reactions but that is another matter entirely.

One offered explanation of why we require a free act known
to be an offence is that by so doing we secure two advantages.[28]
Members of society are able to determine by their choices, at
least to a considerable extent, what their futures will be. They
are able, that is, to opt for law-abidance and its consequences
or disobedience to law and its possible consequences. Thus
there are considerable satisfactions to be gained: individuals
can *enjoy a particular security*, one that would be denied them
under some system which did not make their own choices the
determinants of their futures. The satisfactions of security are,
essentially, satisfactions which accrue from confidence in

26. Hart, *Punishment and Responsibility*, p. 37.
27. pp. 69–70.
28. *Op. cit.*, p. 44 ff.

prediction. I can rule out the possibility of at least certain unpleasant surprises if I feel capable of keeping the law. There are also gains of another kind. That *I* choose what will happen to me, to some considerable extent, is itself a source of satisfaction. In order to see this clearly, one need simply compare the experience of choosing with the experience of, say, being coerced.

It seems undeniable that we have here one recommendation of a punishment system which requires that those punished have performed free actions known to be offences. It is not the only recommendation of such a system, however. There is, as we have seen,[29] an argument to be had from reflection on the experience of apprehended offenders as against victims. There can hardly be any question but that a man who chose not to offend will be more distressed by victimisation than an offender who has done just that. One's being victimised would in no way be a matter of one's own prediction and could not but produce a unique shock, anxiety, and indeed suffering. Indeed, it may be thought that this is an argument against victimisation stronger than the arguments having to do with the satisfactions of choosing and prediction.

Both arguments, it should be noticed, defend the requirement of a more or less deliberate offence as something that helps to secure prevention *at an economical rate*.[30] Is there anything else to be said for the requirement? It is usually thought that there is some recommendation of the requirement which has nothing to do with any of the consequences just mentioned. Consider again a choice between a punishment and a victimisation, where each would have the same preventive effect and no more distress would be caused to the victim than to the offender. Suppose, furthermore, that the victimisation would have no effect on future satisfactions deriving from prediction and choosing. Clearly enough, there is never likely to be such a case, but it is certainly conceivable. Would there, in this instance, be anything to be said for punishment rather than victimisation in virtue of the fact that only the offender had freely and respon-

29. See pp. 71–3.
30. Cf. p. 48, *op. cit.*

sibly chosen to offend? There is a tendency to answer yes. I take it, however, that in so far as one can find 'reasons' for one's inclination, they consist in a refusal to accept the case as specified. That is, one has in mind some respect in which the consequences of the punishment would be preferable to the consequences of the victimisation. There seems nothing to be said for the bare fact in itself that the offender voluntarily offended.

It may be that this is denied as a part of the doctrine we have been considering. There is said to be a moral principle to the effect that 'no one should be punished who could not help doing what he did'.[31] It seems to be implied that a voluntary act, taken by itself and with no regard for consequences, is of moral importance. It is also observed that:

> Human society is a society of persons; and persons do not view themselves or each other merely as so many bodies moving in ways which are sometimes harmful and have to be prevented or altered. Instead persons interpret each other's movements as manifestations of intentions and choices, and these subjective factors are often more important to their social relations than the movements by which they are manifested or their effects. If one person hits another, the person struck does not think of the other as *just* a cause of pain to him; for it is of crucial importance to him whether the blow was deliberate or involuntary. . . . If you strike me, the judgement that the blow was deliberate will elicit fear, indignation, anger, resentment: these are not voluntary responses; but the same judgement will enter into deliberations about my future voluntary conduct towards you and will colour all my social relations with you. Shall I be your friend or enemy? Offer soothing words? Or return the blow? All this will be different if the blow is not voluntary. This is how human nature in human society actually is and as yet we have no power to alter it. The bearing of this fundamental fact on the law is this. If as our legal moralists maintain it is important for the law to reflect common judgement of

31. *Op. cit.*, p. 39.

morality, it is surely even more important that it should in general reflect in its judgements on human conduct distinctions which not only underly morality, but pervade the whole of our social life. This it would fail to do if it treated men merely as alterable, predictable, curable, or manipulable things.[32]

We certainly do distinguish between those who injure us deliberately, those who injure us involuntarily, and, one may add, those who do not injure us at all. We act differently in response. In so far as we are justified in so doing, however, this may be explained by something other than the mere fact that some injuries are the consequences of voluntary actions. What can be said for acts of blaming may be what can be said for certain punishments. The fact taken by itself that an act was voluntary may not in itself be morally important in either case.

Let us grant that in ordinary life we do often act differently, and quite spontaneously, simply and solely because an act was voluntary. It is also true, certainly, that we have distinctive emotional responses. Is it suggested, on the basis of these facts, that the bare consideration that a man has freely offended gives us a moral reason for punishment? Such a suggestion, in my view, would be mistaken. We may be able to give a partial explanation of a feature of our practice of punishment by reference to these facts. Nothing is more likely than that there will be a connection between that practice and our ordinary attitudes and behaviour. To concede that is not to concede the point at issue.

It is not to concede that the fact, taken by itself, that a man has freely and responsibly acted in a certain way is of moral relevance to the question of our further action. Certain responses which we ordinarily have to a person we regard as responsible for his behaviour, responses described in the preceding chapter as moral ones, are not of importance to the determination of our subsequent conduct. A conclusion of a related kind is espoused by some as a consequence of an acceptance of

32. *Op. cit.*, pp. 182–3. Cf. Nigel Walker, *The Aims of a Penal System* (James Seth Memorial Lecture, 1966).

162 PUNISHMENT: THE SUPPOSED JUSTIFICATIONS

determinism. This is a very different route. We have come to our conclusion by reflection on moral attitudes as they are, not as a result of commitment to doctrine.

Before drawing a final conclusion about all of what may be said in justification of punishment, we must consider the other large controversy: strict liability and related procedures. Are we sometimes justified in punishing individuals who do not deserve it, individuals who did *not* voluntarily act in contravention of a system of offences and penalties? The question arises in connection with strict and vicarious liability and in a slightly different way with exemplary penalties. It arises, too, as a consequence of the judicial doctrine of objective liability, which I shall not consider.[33]

The extension of rules of strict liability to cover more and more offences has given rise to a considerable controversy, as indeed it should have. Few things can be said briefly and safely on the subject, and it may be that for a philosopher to venture into it is foolhardy. Still, something is required. What I shall say will be for the most part derivative. One certainty is that it is very nearly impossible to define even the present limits of strict liability. In almost every case a court rather than a legislature has decided that a particular offence is to be tried under rules of strict liability. This itself, in democratic societies, raises a considerable and difficult question. It appears to be possible that almost any statute which does not actually mention intention or negligence in connection with the prohibited act may be construed by a court as allowing for conviction where such things are absent. A study of the law of the state of Wisconsin suggested that of 1,113 statutes creating criminal offences, 660 were so written as to allow courts to convict in the absence of intentionality or negligence if they so desired.[34] This would require only further use of increasingly familiar principles of statute interpretation.

33. See Hart, *op. cit.*, pp. 38–40, etc.
34. Colin Howard, *Strict Responsibility* (London, 1963), p. 7; other discussions of strict liability are to be found in Glanville Williams, *Criminal Law, the General Part*, Second Edition (London, 1961), and Jerome Hall, *General Principles of Criminal Law*, Second Edition (New York, 1960).

Offences where strict liability *may* be the rule, some of which
have been mentioned already, include these:

1. selling adulterated food, selling whisky to a man already
   drunk, labelling food products in a misleading way, giving
   short weight of certain commodities,
2. driving dangerously, not having adequate accident insur-
   ance, having an unsafe vehicle, disobeying traffic regula-
   tions,
3. contraventions of factory safety acts and of wages acts,
4. sexual offences having to do with girls under the age of
   sixteen, and the offence of bigamy,
5. possessing an altered passport, infringing building regula-
   tions, acting in contempt of court, transporting gambling
   equipment, engaging in certain kinds of banking and
   financial transactions, possessing drugs.

It is sometimes said, not merely in defence of strict liability as
we have it but in support of an extension of strict liability to
cover *all* offences, that this is the logical consequence of a
rejection of retributivism. If the rightful function of the courts
is not to 'punish the wicked' but to prevent offences, there can
be no objection to the multiplication of offences of strict liability.
'If the law says that certain things are not to be done, it is
illogical to confine this prohibition to occasions on which they
are done from malice aforethought; for at least the material
consequences of an action, and the reasons for prohibiting it,
are the same whether it is the result of sinister malicious
plotting, of negligence, or of sheer accident.'[35] This can hardly be
acceptable. The rightful function of the courts is not merely to
prevent offences, but to do so in an acceptable way. As I have
suggested already, and will again, one way of achieving
economy of distress in the prevention of offences is by taking
into account the responsibility of defendants. One need not, in
order to oppose strict liability or its extension, advocate traditional retributivism or indeed any retributivism. One may
oppose it, if I may use the words of one advocate, on the ground
that the object of sentencing a man 'should be to take *the*

35. Barbara Wootton, *Crime and the Criminal Law* (London, 1963), p. 51.

minimum action which offers an adequate prospect of preventing future offences'.[36]

A more common argument for strict liability has a number of premisses. It is said to be difficult to prove responsibility with respect to the offences in question. Can one *establish* that a motorist was negligent, that a barman did know the man buying whisky was already drunk, that the seducer did know the girl to be under sixteen? Sometimes the difficulty is located, so to speak, in the nature of things. Sometimes it is maintained that it is extremely difficult or impossible to prove responsibility given our present machinery of justice and the resources which we allot to it. A second premiss must be that it is very necessary that we prevent offences of the kinds in question. There are very extensive dangers to be avoided. Thirdly, it is often maintained that the penalties imposed as a consequence of strict-liability convictions are light ones, at least if one takes into account the resources of offenders. It is said that penalties for motorists under strict-liability rules are manageable ones; larger penalties for prohibited financial transactions can be afforded by those who engage in them. The conclusion is that we are sometimes justified in punishing those who may not have voluntarily offended.

Each of these premisses may be called into question. Can it be shown with respect to all strict-liability offences that it is *more* difficult to prove negligence or intention than with offences where strict liability does not obtain? In some of the latter cases, where proof of negligence *is* required, it is often a relatively easy task. Presumably there is not great difficulty in establishing the negligence of a workman who throws something from the roof of a building into a busy street. But what of proving that a man knew he was receiving stolen goods? There are many cases, surely, where proof is difficult indeed. (An advocate of the extension of strict liability to *all* offences may maintain that proof is in general difficult or even not possible at all by rational means. The argument for this conclusion appears to me to consist in an unwarranted extrapolation from cases whose difficulty cannot be denied. There are motoring

36. *Op. cit.*, p. 95. My italics.

offences, certainly, where the establishment of negligence is or would be a very considerable undertaking. It may well be, to mention another group of cases, extremely difficult to deal adequately with claims having to do with insanity and mental abnormality.[37] This seems an insufficient ground for the general conclusion that is drawn.)

Secondly, is it true that all strict-liability offences, against others where there are the normal requirements of proof, are *peculiarly* dangerous, *peculiarly* in need of deterrence? Can this be made out with respect to the mentioned sexual offences, or action in contempt of court, or possessing an altered passport? One suspects that there is a better argument, despite some curious attitudes to them, with respect to certain motoring offences. Finally, to pass on to the third premiss, is it at all obvious that all the strict-liability penalties are relatively light ones? There are certainly men who would suffer very considerably as a consequence of being convicted of going to bed with a girl under sixteen. There are also small shopkeepers whose trade may be seriously affected by a conviction in connection with adulterated food. *Some* motorists whose penalties include suspension of their driving licences can hardly be regarded as having been lightly penalised. In almost all of these cases, further, it will be thought that convictions must really be deserved, and the usual opprobrium will attach to them. It may sometimes be made clear by the sentencing judge that it is possible or probable, or even something like established, that the defendant did not intend the offence and was not negligent. This will not prevent people in general from supposing otherwise when they hear of a conviction in a criminal court. (Such facts as this, incidentally, have led to suggestions that offences under strict-liability rules should not be called crimes but rather 'quasi-crimes' or 'administrative misdemeanours' or 'violations'.) Against such considerations, the supporter of strict liability might put the following argument. It is not the case that the penalties in question are unfair since, in effect, those who are penalised are selected by something like a random method. They are selected, if in fact they did not intend

37. *Op. cit.*, Chapters Two and Three.

to offend and were not negligent, on the basis of accident. If there is a need for deterring punishments and if we cannot satisfy it by punishing those who deserve it, what fairer method than this? The argument is not one to be found in legal writing, I think, for understandable reasons, but it is a coherent one for all of that. Its weakness is obviously that it depends on assumptions about which there can be considerable doubt. *Is* there such a need for deterring penalties? *Is* it true that we cannot deter as much as we need by punishing those who voluntarily offend? It is only if these things are positively established that we should approve of the suggested method.

It is patently impossible, on the basis of what can be said here, to draw any firm conclusions about all of the offences where strict liability is in question. My own inclination is that with respect to *most* of them, neither the dangers to be avoided nor the difficulties in proving responsibility are so great as to warrant treating individuals as they may not deserve. It is difficult to resist the supposition that strict liability is a fact not so much as a consequence of the given arguments but because of some retributivist determination that none of the guilty should escape. With respect to *some* of the offences in question, where there is a large danger to be avoided, there may be a justification for a recommended alteration in judicial procedure.[38] We might, with respect to these, distinguish penalties in some way as to their weight. This would be a difficult but neither an impossible nor an unfamiliar task. In the case of heavy penalties there should be a strict adherence to the principle that the responsibility of defendants be proved by the prosecution. In the case of relatively light penalties, the procedure would be different. It would not be necessary for the prosecution to prove the accused acted with intention or negligence. However, it would be possible for a man to escape conviction by he himself showing, perhaps on balance of probabilities, that he did not intend the offence and was not negligent. Such a practice would decrease very considerably the incidence of undeserved punishments. It would not rule

38. See Howard, *Strict Responsibility*. Cf. Hart, *Punishment and Responsibility*, Chapter Eight.

them out. The argument is that the relatively few undeserved penalties which would be imposed would be justified by the gain in the prevention of dangerous offences. It seems possible that a similar system would be defensible for offences now governed by vicarious liability.

There remains the question of exemplary penalties. Here there is usually no question of a man's being punished who was in no way responsible for the action in question. Exemplary penalties may none the less be regarded as penalties which are in a particular sense not deserved. They are penalties greater than those imposed on other similar offenders. The matter presents difficulties because of the vagueness of the requirement that similar offenders be treated in similar ways. Certainly it is the case that judges ought not to depart from the penalty limitations laid down by statute for particular kinds of offence. A penalty not within the specified range is certainly unjustified. There is room within the range, however, for a good deal of choice, and there has often been a wide variance in sentencing from court to court. Some penalties *permitted* by statute may be undeserved, it seems, in that the offenders in question are more severely penalised than others. They are more severely penalised than others who have committed offences of similar harmfulness and responsibility. Is there a justification for sometimes departing from the rule that offenders similar in this respect are to be treated similarly? The argument advanced is that sometimes there is a need for an unusual deterrent. It seems to me impossible to assert that we should *never* be influenced by this consideration. At the same time, it seems more than arguable that many exemplary penalties are not open to justification in this way.

7. *Conclusions*

Implicit in what has been said in this chapter and before is a conclusion about the justification of a possible practice of punishment or, better, a practice of punishment in a possible society. I should like to make this conclusion explicit, to clarify it in several ways, and also to examine certain implica-

M

tions. There will remain other questions, including that of the justification of our practices in our societies as they are, and that of what principles must govern the assessment of these practices. These are more important questions and their answers are also implicit in the foregoing.

The conclusion can be summarised in this way. Punishments may be justified when they are economically preventive of offences and in a certain sense deserved. They may sometimes be justified when they are *not* deserved. Let us for the moment ignore cases of the second kind, which may be regarded as rare.

What we then have, more specifically, is that punishments may be justified when (1) they are economically preventive of offences, (2) those individuals punished have voluntarily acted in ways which contravened a known system of offences and penalties, (3) they are punished as other similar offenders are punished, (4) their penalties contribute to an equalisation of welfare and distress with regard to offenders and non-offenders, and (5) their penalties do not produce situations of gross inequality of distress. This last requirement was omitted, or not specifically mentioned, in the doctrine considered at the beginning of the preceding section. It is included because we would not regard as justified an economical punishment which avoided small amounts of distress for each of very many people at the cost of a great deal of distress for a single individual.

This claim, obviously, is misleadingly and inefficiently formulated. We have accepted that partly to justify a punishment by the fact that the offender responsibly and knowingly offended is to justify it as in a way economical. For one thing, it is productive of less distress than would be caused to someone who was penalised although he had not responsibly and knowingly offended. The second stated requirement for a justified punishment, then, is no more than a repetition of something implicit in the first. What of the third, fourth, and fifth requirements?

The fourth is that penalties imposed must at least contribute to an equalisation of welfare and distress with respect to offenders and non-offenders. What I wish to suggest is that the third and fifth requirements are in a way consequences of the fourth. Let us suppose that we have a society where there exists very considerable equality of welfare and distress. This equality is disrupted by the commission of offences. Penalties can be imposed which will indeed have the feature that they contribute to an equalisation. That is, they at least tend to re-establish the state of affairs that existed before the commission of offences. In their offences, it may be argued, offenders gained satisfactions and others were deprived. In the ensuing punishments the balance is righted. Penalties which have this feature, of course, are necessarily penalties which fulfil the fifth requirement: they do not produce situations of gross inequality of distress. Given that the punishments are to re-establish equality, further, we have the consequence that offenders who are alike in a certain respect must be treated in like ways. We have the conclusion, more particularly, that offenders who have gained like satisfactions from their offences should receive like punishments. Only by doing this can we return to the society of equality. (There is, of course, another way in which one might interpret the requirement that like offenders be treated alike. It may be regarded as the necessity that offenders who have caused a similar harm, and by actions of a similar degree of responsibility, should be treated alike. In this case, what we have is something that follows in different ways from the initial requirement of economical prevention.)

Given these considerations we can produce a simpler and clearer form of our conclusion about *the justification of a practice of punishment in a possible society. It would be an absolute requirement of such a practice that it prevented offences at an economical cost of distress. It would at least in general be the case, if this was achieved, that punishment was of those individuals responsible for actions contravening a known system of offences and penalties. It would also be an absolute requirement that the penalties would re-establish equality of satisfactions and distress.*

In the supposed society of equality, it seems, certain penalties will satisfy both these requirements. If Green commits an offence, and gains certain satisfactions from it, the penalty suggested by considerations of economical deterrence will be one which makes for the re-establishment of equality. This, however, is precisely what is not true of punishment in our societies as they are. Given that they are societies of extreme or considerable inequality, and that to some large extent offenders come from deprived classes or groups, punishing them will contribute to inequality rather than equality. That is, a large proportion of those punished have already been subjected to unequal treatment: even taking into account satisfactions got from offences they have already had a larger share of distress and a lesser share of welfare than other members of society. The penalties they are given will make a further contribution to this inequality. The conclusion to which we have come, then, is that there is a justification which a practice of punishment in a conceivable society might have, a justification suggested by several of the doctrines we have considered. It is *not* a justification which can be given for practices of punishment in our societies as they are.

The best that can be claimed of our existing practices is (1) *that they sometimes prevent offences at an economical rate, partly because in general the individuals punished are those responsible for offences, and* (2) *that the penalties do make a certain contribution to the avoidance of inequality.* It seems to me very arguable that many of our punishments are not economical. Some that come to mind are the very common short prison sentences for minor offences and particularly severe penalties for certain dramatic crimes. One thinks also of penalties for certain broad classes of offences. It has often been maintained with good reason that offences against property, as distinct for example from offences against the person, are penalised in an unacceptably severe way. Again, there is some very considerable question about repeated punishment of chronic offenders: the greater the number of previous court appearances, the more likely it is that a man will offend again.[39] One cannot but suppose that a considerable number of penalties are uneconomical, finally, simply because of the extremely unsettling variation in sentences for the same

39. W. H. Hammond and E. Chayen, *Persistent Criminals* (London, 1963).

offence between different courts.[40] To establish that many of our penalties are economical, however, would require a detailed and careful investigation of a particularity and kind that cannot be attempted here. To establish that many of our penalties do have a sufficient deterrent effect would also require such an investigation. This also is in question in certain cases.

Let us say that *some* of our punishments do function as economical deterrents. Our practice, as I have said, may have another recommendation claimed for it. It must be admitted that it often contributes to inequality. None the less, it can be seen in another light if one considers certain alternative situations. That is, it may be maintained that a society *very like ours,* except that it lacked the practice of punishment, would involve *even greater inequality*. It is important that this contention be put in this way. It is important that we have in mind an alternative society which like our present ones involves very considerable inequality, aggressiveness, acquisitiveness, and a number of other features. The point here is that we should not drift in the direction of a certain position of unreality. There is very little to be said for some such defence of our practice of punishment as this one: *any* society which lacked a practice of punishment would involve even more inequality than our present one. There is very little to be said either for or against such a claim. To dismiss or to embrace it, in any rational way, is an impossibility given our present state of knowledge.[41] We know too little, to mention but one large area of speculation, of the effect of possible societal institutions on what is called human nature. Utopian conceptions of society and their dismissals, in their many forms, must be regarded as what they are: speculations and pointers to experiment, not premises for practical argument of any general kind.

Given things as they are, and as they are likely to be for the foreseeable future, there is a defence for some punishments.

40. Roger Hood, *Sentencing in Magistrates' Courts* (London, 1962).
41. Crime, in our societies, is very largely the work of males. That females do not offend anything like so much is to be explained in large part by cultural factors. Would a more pervasively 'feminine' society, if it lacked a practice of punishment, involve greater inequalities than ours?

It is that they do prevent what we wish to avoid, and that they do so at a reasonable price. They do not cause more distress than would occur without them, and they are a means of avoiding even greater inequality than we have. It may be objected that these conclusions require much more than has been provided by way of factual argument. This is, alas, a thoroughly reasonable objection. That punishment does in a considerable number of cases have a deterring effect seems to me adequately established. That it does so economically in many of the same cases seems to me true but not established here. That it ensures a lesser inequality seems also true and also not established here. That our punishing should be governed by a vastly greater hesitancy seems true and less in need of establishment.

Answers of a kind, then, have been given to two of the questions mentioned at the beginning of this section. There remains this: By what tests should we decide the moral acceptability of practices of punishment in our societies? What principles should direct more particular investigations of their justification? The answer, which does seem to me established, is that *acceptable practices must prevent offences at the lowest possible cost of distress, and certainly not by causing more distress than would occur without them. Furthermore, they must not themselves give rise to excessive inequality, but rather secure that more equality or less inequality obtains than would obtain in their absence.* It is not a *fundamental* requirement of the moral acceptability of a practice of punishment that those who are punished deserve it, where this means essentially that they have freely and responsibly offended.

That men deserve punishment is not by itself a sufficient justification. Retributivism is a mistake. It is not sufficient that punishment deter economically, or that it reforms men. Both the traditional deterrence theory and the theories of reform are mistaken. Finally, to turn to the typical compromise theory, it is not a sufficient justification that punishment is economically preventive and also deserved, if the latter means no more than that it is imposed on individuals responsible for offences. To say this, as we have seen, is not really to advance separate considerations in justification. What *can* justify punishment is the reduction of distress at an economical rate, usually to be obtained by imposing penalties on those responsible for offences, and the fact, if it is one, that the practice contributes to the avoidance of greater inequality.

6

Liberty and Punishment

1. *Mill*

WE have come to a conclusion about what may justify punishments in our societies. In so doing, we have given an answer of a kind to another question. If we assume, as seems reasonable, that only those actions should be crimes which may justifiably be punished, we have some answer to the question of what actions should be illegal, should be crimes. It is a familiar fact of political and social philosophy that a closely related question, about what actions should *not* be crimes, has long been a subject of controversy. Or, if that is not quite true, there has long been controversy about a slightly wider question. What limits should be set to the intervention of the state and society in the lives of individuals? What should be left to individuals, without fear either of criminal prosecution or coercion in any other form? This has long been discussed without reference to the problem of the justification of punishment. I should now like, by way of undeveloped postscript, to bring together these two areas of dispute. That they *are* connected can hardly be denied.

Doctrines about State and societal intervention, or those that are interesting given a prior commitment to democracy, can best be approached through Mill's essay, *On Liberty*. It remains true, oddly, that his central principle is still thought to be precisely enunciated in the following passage.

. . . the sole end for which mankind are warranted, either individually or collectively, in interfering with the liberty of action of any of their number, is self-protection . . . the only purpose for which power can be rightfully exercised over any member of a civilised community, against his will, is to prevent harm to others. His own good, either physical or moral, is not a sufficient warrant. He cannot rightfully be compelled to do or forbear because it will be better for him to do so, because it will make him happier, because, in the opinions of others, to do so would be wise, or even right.[1]

Mill has in mind the exercise of coercion by private members of society and groups, mainly but not only in the form of 'public opinion', and also punishment by the State. If we restrict ourselves to the latter, his claim here appears to be that punishment *may* be justified when a man harms others by his actions and can never be justified on the grounds merely that his actions are taken to be immoral or to be harmful to himself. That is, there is a possibility that punishment is justified in the one case, and none in the other.[2] Since *On Liberty* appeared, the most common criticism has been that Mill's doctrine rests on a simple mistake and thus is pointless. Its main intention is to exclude the State from a certain area of life, which may be more fully described as that one in which individuals do not harm anyone, even themselves, or harm only themselves, or harm certain others only with their full consent and agreement. The others in question, agreeing partners as I shall call them, must be 'of full age and not forced or deceived'.[3] The supposed mistake consists in thinking that there are any actions which harm only an individual or agreeing partners and nobody else.

The solitary drunkard or drug addict, consenting homosexuals, pimps and their customers, procurers of abortions, anyone who commits an act of euthanasia or attempts to commit suicide—all these individuals and many others who offend against customary morality are assumed by Mill's critics to be harming

1. *On Liberty*, in *Utilitarianism* (London, 1962), edited by Mary Warnock, p. 135.
2. *Op. cit.*, p. 227.
3. *Op. cit.*, p. 138.

themselves or their agreeing partners. It is supposed that this is not something from which Mill would in any way dissent. However, it is argued, it is just a mistake to suppose that in all these contraventions of morality, only agents and partners are harmed. The addict makes himself incapable of contributing to society and so harms us all. Also, others may be influenced by him and so become addicts. Furthermore, there are indirect effects on other moral and social standards. In general, there are no merely self-harming actions: actions, that is, that harm only the agent and any agreeing partners. It appears to be supposed that Mill was oblivious of this supposed truth. When it is seen, we are told, his doctrine must be regarded as consummately self-defeating. Its intention is to exclude the State from a quite considerable part of individual life. It succeeds only in excluding the State from uncontroversial activities which harm nobody at all.[4]

This view of *On Liberty* must often have been the product of not having read it. In the third paragraph after that one which contains the passage quoted above, Mill reiterates that the State is to be excluded from 'all that portion of a person's life and conduct which affects only himself, or, if it also affects others, only with their free, voluntary and undeceived consent and participation'. He then adds:

> When I say only himself, I mean directly, and in the first instance, for whatever affects himself, may affect others through himself; and the objections which may be grounded on this contingency will receive consideration in the sequel.[5]

He does in a later section consider the objection that there are no merely self-harming actions, in the sense defined above. Furthermore, he chooses explicitly to admit it.[6] What, then, *is* 'the one very simple principle' which he intends and which he

4. That this has been what amounts to the orthodox view of Mill is shown, for example, by J. C. Rees, in 'A Rereading of Mill On Liberty', *Political Studies*, 1960, p. 113.
5. Mill, *op. cit.*, p. 137.
6. *Op. cit.*, p. 210 ff.

too vaguely states in the earlier parts of his essay? One answer that has been given[7] is that Mill intends to distinguish between two kinds of harm that may result from an individual's action, two kinds in addition to the harm caused to the agent himself and any agreeing partners. The distinction between these two kinds of harm is made by way of the idea of interests or rights.

To say a man has certain interests, in the relevant sense, is to say that if he is harmed in certain ways he has a right of redress. These interests, we are told in this interpretation of Mill, are those which 'depend for their existence on social recognition and are closely connected with prevailing standards about the sort of behaviour a man can legitimately expect from others.'[8] To take an obvious case, ownership of property gives rise to interests. If my property is damaged by others under certain circumstances, I can make some recovery under existing law. We have the notions, then, of harm to individuals which involves injury to interests and harm to individuals which does not involve injury to their interests. Harm of the first sort gives rise to a right of redress; harm of the second sort does not. The suggestion is that Mill's intention was to advance this principle: The State may possibly be justified in intervening whan a man harms another, who is not an agreeing partner, and in so doing injures his interests. Mill does write in one place that 'for such actions as are prejudicial to the interests of others, the individual is accountable, and may be subjected either to social or to legal punishment, if society is of the opinion that the one or the other is requisite for its protection'.[9]

This interpretation has a considerable advantage over its predecessors. Even given the assumptions about the harmfulness of all supposed immorality and the impossibility of actions harming only agents and partners, Mill's principle is not useless. For example, it does appear to exclude the state from interference with a drug addict, who might be said to harm others in

7. Rees, *op. cit.* A new postscript was added to the paper on republication in *Limits of Liberty* (Belmont, California, 1966), edited by Peter Radcliff.

8. *Op. cit.*, p. 119.

9. *Op. cit.*, p. 226.

indirect ways, perhaps through his failure to contribute to society, but cannot be said to injure any established interests of others. There is, I think, a tenable distinction between harming a man, simply, and harming him in such a way as to injure his interests. It should be noticed, however, that the two notions are not so different as may be supposed. The relevant notion of a man's being harmed is not purely a descriptive one. If I am harmed, I am deprived of something desirable to which I have *some* claim or reasonable expectation. (I am not harmed if I am deprived of something I have stolen.) I may be deprived of something to which I have *some* claim, however, without its being correct to say that interests of mine have been injured. That is, I may have nothing very like a right of redress. It might be said, if the words are in place, that the distinction between harm and harm involving injury to interests is one of degree rather than kind. My use of the word 'harm' at this point, obviously, is a wide one, considerably wider than the notion of harm within the law.

None the less, if this version of Mill's principle does not have the disability of the traditional and mistaken one, there are other things to be said against it. The principle so construed, as has been argued,[10] is essentially conservative, protective of the *status quo*, since the extent of state action in the controversial area is determined by what are actually established, legally or socially, as interests. Given this, it cannot reflect Mill's intention. It is not in accord with the tenor of his thought[11] or

---

10. By Richard Wollheim in an unpublished paper of which a reduced version appears in *Man and Society*, No. 6, 1963. Professor Wollheim's own reading of Mill, which I consider below, is stated in this version. Cf. C. L. Ten, 'Mill on Self-Regarding Actions', *Philosophy*, 1968.

11. Wollheim writes: '. . . it is an undoubted fact, clear from various sources such as the essays on Bentham and Coleridge, the *Autobiography* and the sixth book of the *System of Logic*, that Mill in his general thinking about politics was torn between the universalistic liberal approach typical of the 18th Century and the particularistic conservative approach typical of the 19th Century. But in *On Liberty* he surely takes his stand unambiguously on the side of the tradition in which he was brought up rather than on that of the new thinking with which, as he tells us in the *Autobiography*, he tried to correct his own intellectual balance.'

with specific recommendations in *On Liberty* that the state
should not be barred from interference with behaviour
simply because the behaviour in question does not endanger or
damage interests of a recognised kind. There is also another
related disability. Mill makes it clear that he regards whatever
principle he intends as based on the Principle of Utility, albeit
not in quite Jeremy Bentham's sense.[12] But the version of the
intervention principle under discussion does not derive from the
Principle of Utility. Indeed, it appears to be inconsistent with
it. It could be consistent with it only if the interests in question,
those which were legally and socially recognised in Mill's
time, were precisely those enjoined by the Principle of Utility.
There was not this identity, and Mill did not suppose that
there was.

What principle, then, should we take him to have intended?
That question, perhaps, does not really express the necessary
nature of our inquiry. Given the inconsistencies of *On Liberty*,
it requires a certain piety to think that Mill did have clear
in his mind some exact principle which he failed to formulate
adequately. We might better ask, I think, to what Mill is committed, given several fixed points, most importantly his
Principle of Utility.

Another answer[13] to one of these questions is the principle,
briefly stated, that the State may not intervene with respect to
actions which harm others than the agent and partners if this
harm arises solely by way of the beliefs of those individuals. It

12. Mill writes in *Utilitarianism* (*op. cit.*, p. 257): 'The creed which
accepts as the foundation of morals, Utility, or the Greatest Happiness
Principle, holds that actions are right as they tend to promote happiness,
wrong as they tend to produce the reverse of happiness. By happiness is
intended pleasure, and the absence of pain; by unhappiness, pain, and the
privation of pleasure.' Cf. my statement above, p. 74. Mill writes in *On
Liberty* (*op. cit.*, p. 136): 'I regard utility as the ultimate appeal on all
ethical questions; but it must be utility in the largest sense, grounded on
the permanent interests of man as a progressive being. Those interests, I
contend, authorise the subjection of individual spontaneity to external
control, only in respect to those actions of each which concern the interest of
other people.'

13. Wollheim, *op. cit.*

is in general true that Mill did wish to exclude the State from interference in activities which may be said to cause harm only via beliefs, such as Sunday sport which offends the sensibilities of Sabbatarians. To make Mill's principle only this, however, would raise an obvious difficulty. It would not serve to exclude the state in such cases as that of the discreet drug addict. The supposed harm he causes to others, by failing to contribute to society, does not depend on their beliefs if any about the wrongfulness of taking drugs. An attempt is made to meet this difficulty in the following way. Mill's principle, whatever it is, depends on classifying actions in terms of their consequences. A preliminary question, then, is what things are to count at all as consequences of action. In particular, suppose I do A rather than B, and X would have followed had I done B. Is the non-occurrence of X to be regarded as a consequence of my doing A? It is suggested that Mill's answer to this preliminary question is that the non-occurrence of X counts as a consequence of my doing A if this non-occurrence occasions perceptible hurt to an assignable individual or is such that I may be said to have failed in a specific duty to the public.

I wish to suggest two of a number of difficulties involved in this interpretation of Mill. (1) What we have when more fully stated is the principle that the State may not intervene in a man's behaviour if some harm cannot rightly be counted as a consequence of his actions, or if a harm which is a consequence arises by way of the beliefs of the person harmed. The first part of the principle may be taken to exclude the State from interference with the addict. That is, he may not have failed in a specific duty to the public or caused perceptible hurt to an assignable individual. The second part of the principle excludes the State from interference in cases like that one involving the offended Sabbatarian. (The State is also excluded, of course, by *this* part of the principle, from interference with the indiscreet addict who *is* said to cause harm by way of the beliefs of those harmed.) It is the first part of the principle that seems to me unacceptable. How are we to determine when a man has performed an action such that the ensuing harm is a consequence of the action? One *might* concede that whether or not perceptible hurt has been caused to an assignable individual is a question to be settled by consideration of the facts. One might concede, more precisely, that it is neither an evaluative question nor one concerned with prevailing norms and standards. Such a concession cannot be made with respect to the question of when a man has failed in a specific duty to the public. This question, under an ordinary interpretation, is one to be settled by consideration of prevailing norms and standards and, in particular, consideration of the law.[14] Given this, however, the principle which is being advanced is in one crucial part conservative in effect and quite likely inconsistent with the Principle of Utility. The principle in one important part shares the disability of the one previously considered. (2) It can hardly be taken as the principle intended by Mill. It cannot be reconciled with his many formulations which do not mention belief-dependent harms or his failure explicitly to mention in *On Liberty* the essential definition of consequences.

2. *Reinterpretation*

I wish now to offer another view of the essay.[15] It is certainly true that it was a part of Mill's desire to state a principle incorporating the notion of interests in connection with harm caused to others than agents and agreeing partners. A reading of his fourth chapter, in which after an explicit discussion he agrees that self-harming actions also harm others, can leave no doubt of this.[16] What is not true, however, is that we must understand the interests in question simply as those actually recognised or established by society. At the beginning of the fourth chapter Mill very much gives the impression that he has come to the point of providing the canonical form of his

14. Another answer, but not one suggested by Wollheim, is that the duties in question are those sanctioned by the Principle of Utility. Difficulties which attach to an answer of this kind are considered below in connection with what I take to be the most defensible reading of Mill's essay.

15. A part of what I have to say in this section, and of what I have said already, appears in my article, 'Mill on Liberty', *Inquiry*, 1967.

16. Perhaps this is too strong a claim. Cf. Ten, *op. cit.*

principle. He writes that each citizen, if his liberty is not to be intruded upon by the State, must follow a certain line of conduct toward others.

> This conduct consists, first, in not injuring the interests of one another; or rather certain interests, which, either by express legal provision or tacit understanding, *ought to be* considered as rights; and secondly, in each person bearing his share (to be fixed on some equitable principle) of the labours and sacrifices incurred for defending the society or its members from injury and molestation.[17]

What I wish to point out, of course, is that the interests in question are here specifically *not* identified with those interests which 'depend for their existence on social recognition and are closely connected with prevailing standards about the sort of behaviour a man can legitimately expect from others'. Mill's principle as here stated is essentially this: the State may not interfere unless a man's actions injure what ought to be accepted as the interests or rights of others, whether or not they are so accepted. What is the test of whether there has been damage to what ought to be regarded as a man's interests, as harm which ought to give him a right of redress? For Mill the test must be the Principle of Utility. In short, what we have is that the State may not interfere with my behaviour if I do not violate interests of others—those interests sanctioned by the Principle of Utility.

Three things can be said for this understanding. (1) It too escapes the traditional objection that Mill's principle prohibits interference with no behaviour at all other than the kind that is not immoral and causes harm to nobody at all. (2) The principle so understood is not conservative and, to say the least, is consistent with the Principle of Utility. It is evidently the principle to which Mill is committed. (3) It does not much matter, but it may also be regarded as what Mill often intended

17. *On Liberty*, p. 205. My italics. The second requirement stated is for our purposes irrelevant.

or had in mind. The passage I have quoted gives some support to this view. Of course, *On Liberty* falls short of being paralysed by rigour, and Mills' careless *largesse* in enunciations of his position make it possible to find *some* passage that may be so read as to support any reasonable speculation. Two points about his many statements of position may be worth making. With respect to those that mention simply harm to others than the agent and agreeing partners,[18] it is not unreasonable to assume that he had in mind harm to interests. Secondly, it is likely that when he speaks as if his principle does turn on recognised or established interests, he refers to those of them that he regarded as being in accord with Utility. But that the State may possibly intervene only when such interests are damaged is to be explained not by the fact that they are established but rather by the fact that they are in accord with Utility.

When we take Mill's principle to be that the State may not intervene unless what I shall call utility interests of others than the agent and partners are injured or threatened, there is the following objection. The principle so understood certainly fails to fulfil Mill's main hope. It cannot do what he envisaged as its job. More important, *we* must regard it as failing in this respect. Ultimately, Mill wishes to submit all actions, including those of the state, to the judgement of the Principle of Utility. In *On Liberty* his endeavour was to establish 'one very simple principle', of a subordinate nature, with respect to State intervention. This principle would in function be an analogue to the moral principles or rules having to do with truth-telling and promise-keeping. However, it may be objected, the principle we are taking him to have produced obviously *incorporates* the Principle of Utility. What we have is that the State may not intervene if my actions do not injure or endanger those interests of others which are in accord with the Principle of Utility. Any operation of the given principle of intervention, then, involves a use of the Principle of Utility. One must know or ask, in each case, if interests which may be claimed *are* in accord with Utility. Perhaps this could do with fuller explanation. Mill writes in *Utilitarianism* that

18. As suggested by Rees, *op. cit.*, p. 135.

N

184 PUNISHMENT: THE SUPPOSED JUSTIFICATIONS

It is a strange notion that the acknowledgement of a first principle is inconsistent with the admission of secondary ones. . . . The proposition that happiness is the end and aim of morality does not mean that no road ought to be laid down to that goal, or that persons going thither should not be advised to take one direction rather than another. . . . Nobody argues that the art of navigation is not founded on astronomy, because sailors cannot wait to calculate the Nautical Almanack. Being rational creatures they go to sea with it already calculated. . . .[19]

Mill attempts, with respect to the question of State intervention, to provide a useful principle of quite considerable generality and subordinate to the Principle of Utility. To do so, of course, would not simply be to devise a time-saver, but to give an answer to a difficult question about one of the consequences of the Principle of Utility. What we are taking him to have produced, however, is tantamount to the injunction that the State must not intervene when in so doing it would contravene the Principle of Utility.

This is the objection and it cannot be avoided. It will be worth while, however, from several points of view, to consider a possible rejoinder. It may be contended that it is not true that *every* operation of the principle of intervention involves an operation of the Principle of Utility. In many important instances, it may be said, this is not so. Mill's traditional critics suppose that (1) *all* acts generally considered to be immoral are also harmful acts. Individuals and their agreeing partners, if any, harm themselves by engaging in certain behaviour. (2) Furthermore, they harm others. It must be admitted that Mill in some places may appear to accept the first proposition. This is so when he gives his energies to dealing with the second one, and appears not to question the truth of the first. It is a fact, of course, but not to the point, that he does consider a good number of activities generally considered immoral to be harmful. It is an oversight to think that he accepts this of all the activities in question or is in any way committed to accepting

19. *Utilitarianism*, edited by Mary Warnock, p. 276.

it. *On Liberty* is a work of reiterations, and not many things are more often repeated than the claim that orthodox or accepted doctrines and moralities are commonly mistaken. One of the things they may be mistaken about, obviously, is the question of whether or not certain actions and activities are harmful to the people involved. More to the point, Mill rightly believes that in many cases activities commonly taken to be immoral have not been harmful. More or less trivial examples can be had from the dietary rules of some societies. Today, it can certainly be argued that there are sexual actions and activities which are harmless and of which orthodox morality, if it can be located, disapproves. That Mill did distinguish what is ordinarily condemned from what is harmful is a contention that hardly needs support. If it is thought to be needed, it is provided by his hymn to individuality, the third chapter of the essay.

Given this, it may be said, it becomes apparent that the principle of intervention in question does not always, or in all important cases, bring in the Principle of Utility. The intervention principle, alternatively written, is (1) that State may not intervene when an individual's actions are not harmful, and (2) it may not intervene when any harm to others than the agent and partners does not involve injury to utility interests. The second part, it may be said, does have the disability in question but the first part does not. We do then have a principle which does in certain important cases have the function that Mill had in mind.

Unfortunately, this will not work. The reason is the simple one, which may be anticipated, that it is not only a factual question as to whether or not something constitutes a harm. The question calls for an evaluation. As I have said, if I am so affected by an action as to be harmed, my new state must by some standard be an undesirable one. The standard for Mill is obviously the Principle of Utility. What we then have is the conclusion that the principle of State intervention, in both of its parts, does involve the Principle of Utility. Of course it must not be supposed that *On Liberty*, even from what might be called a theoretical or doctrinal point of view, is without

N*

significance. If it fails to provide a useful and fairly general principle of State intervention, it does defend a position which can be clearly stated and also advances certain maxims of very considerable importance. There is, given the Principle of Utility, to be no interference in freedom of thought and expression. There is to be no interference, at least in certain circumstances, when harm caused to an individual comes by way of his own beliefs and would not arise otherwise.

3. *The Enforcement of Morality*

We shall return to Mill's essay, and to what must be his position with respect to individual liberty, but I should like now to define and criticise two other doctrines and to consider a particular controversy. One persistent claim is that a particular morality, a moral code thought to be shared by a society, is of such intrinsic value that the State may be justified in enforcing it on individuals by punishment. The State *may* be justified in interventions not only when individuals in some sense harm others than their agreeing partners, but also when they merely act in what are held to be immoral ways. These latter interventions are justified as means to the end of preserving the morality in question, which is important in itself.[20]

This is related to, if certainly not identical with, the traditional retribution theory of punishment. There is at least a possibility, indeed, that the doctrine of State intervention and the retribution theory of punishment would have different consequences in a particular case. It is at least a possibility that on occasion the punishment of a man who offends against accepted morality, in such a way as to break the law, would not be thought necessary for the preservation of morality. It is conceivable even that it be thought likely to have a harmful effect on that morality. In such a circumstance, presumably, the intervention doctrine and the retribution theory would not issue in compatible conclusions.

20. As pointed out by Hart (*Law, Liberty and Morality* [London, 1963], p. 55), James Fitzjames Stephen advances this doctrine among others in *Liberty, Equality, Fraternity* (London, 1873).

There are a number of quite obvious criticisms of this demand for the enforcement of morality and I shall do no more than mention them.[21] The argument requires that there be a wide assent to the morality which punishment is to preserve. It seems not the case at least in contemporary societies that there is any such consensus. It must be remembered, of course, that we are dealing with such matters as sexual behaviour, abortion, attempted suicide, euthanasia, drunkenness, and drug-taking. Secondly, the argument contains at least one important ambiguity. Is the supposed end in question the securing of something like sincere belief in the accepted morality, a kind of willing commitment to it, or is it merely the end of securing behaviour in accordance with it? The former 'higher' end, I think, has usually been the goal. It is not at all obviously true, however, that the punishment of offenders is likely to secure this effect. One can at best have a number of hypotheses of a doubtful nature, hypotheses providing an indirect connection between the punishment of offenders and the supposed consequences of sincere commitment. Thirdly, one might put aside both these difficulties and yet argue that the distress involved in the punishment of supposed immoralities, which may harm nobody, cannot be justified by attainment of the end in question, however construed. It is important to keep in mind at this point that the end in question is not the prevention of harm. The end is no more than commitment to a particular shared morality or else behaviour in accord with it. The argument is, if anything, less acceptable than the argument for the traditional retribution theory of punishment.

A distinct but related doctrine, which appears also to be opposed to Mill's liberalism, is advanced by one of his recent critics.[22] Its central contention is preserved in this passage.

> . . . it is not possible to set theoretical limits to the power of the state to legislate against immorality. It is not possible to settle in advance exceptions to the general rule or to define inflexibly areas of morality into which the law is in no

21. Some of those I include, as well as others, are advanced by Hart, *op. cit.*
22. Patrick Devlin, *The Enforcement of Morals* (London, 1965).

circumstances to be allowed to enter. Society is entitled by means of its laws to protect itself from dangers, whether from within or without. Here again I think that the political parallel is legitimate. The law of treason is directed against aiding the king's enemies and against sedition from within. The justification for this is that established government is necessary for the existence of society and therefore its safety against violent overthrow must be secured. But an established morality is as necessary as good government to the welfare of society. Societies disintegrate from within more frequently than they are broken up by external pressures. There is disintegration when no common morality is observed and history shows that the loosening of moral bonds is often the first stage of disintegration, so that society is justified in taking the same steps to preserve its moral code as it does to preserve its government and other essential institutions.[23]

The argument here is not that an established or shared morality is something which has such attractions in itself that punishment may be used to preserve it. The argument is rather that a shared morality is a necessary condition of the preservation of society. *That* is unquestionably a good thing, or perhaps it is the preservation of English or American or similar societies that is unquestionably a good thing. What may justify the punishment of certain acts, then, is that punishment may preserve the shared morality of the society, and preserving the morality preserves the society. It is the avoidance of harm on a grand scale that justifies intervention. There is one way, then, in which this doctrine is in agreement with Mill's intentions. In both cases we have an attempt to base a principle of intervention on considerations of harm. Although Mill did not envisage the catastrophic harm we are now asked to consider, the label 'utilitarian' may be applied to both doctrines.

We may here notice what is supposed to be the main distinction between the two doctrines. It is much insisted, in the one we are considering, not that we should at present punish this or that supposed immorality, but that there can be no

23. *Op. cit.*, pp. 12–13.

'theoretical limit' to the State's right of intervention. There may just now be no sufficient reason to legislate against some tupposed sexual immorality, for example. However, should shis immorality become widely practised, we might have sufficient reason. Given this possibility, there can be no acceptance of a doctrine which rules out legislation in advance. It is supposed[24] that there is in Mill a precise contrast to this, an attempt to set a theoretical limit of a certain kind, once and for all, to the State's activities. This involves a confusion. Mill submits that if behaviour of individuals does threaten harm of a certain sort then interference is a possibility. He does not consider the proposition that some behaviour of individuals, generally considered immoral, may threaten the very existence of a society. He would no doubt have agreed, however, that *if* the supposed behaviour were to threaten the existence of a society, and *if* the continued existence of that society had a utilitarian justification, then interference might be justified. Nothing in his argument suggests otherwise. What is closed off is the possibility of intervention when there is no harm, in a certain sense, in question. There is no reason for thinking that this last proposition is inconsistent with the doctrine we are considering. However, the ultimate premises of that doctrine are not made explicit. More to the point, perhaps, there can hardly be an argument to the effect that *no* proposals as to absolute limits on State intervention are acceptable. Could anyone object to the proposal that the State should be regarded as under an absolute prohibition with respect to the pointless degradation of its citizens?

Mill, although he does not consider the point explicitly, is clearly of the opinion that no significant probability attaches to the proposition that society will one day disintegrate or be endangered by the supposed immoralities in question. In this, he is surely right. The weakness of the supposition to the contrary, although on occasion misconstrued by critics, has been adequately indicated.[25] It is a significant probability that a

24. *Op. cit.*, p. 103, p. 113, p. 125.
25. See, on this and other points, Hart, *Law, Liberty and Morality*, and Wollheim, 'Crime, Sin and Mr. Justice Devlin', *Encounter*, 1959.

society will change, in a number of different ways, if certain practices become widespread. There is more than a low probability, no doubt, that English or American societies would eventually change very considerably as a consequence of a widespread practice of euthanasia. However, there is no reason whatever to confuse change in a society with the society's being destroyed or its existence being endangered. The vague proposition that the *existence* of a society may be endangered by departures from a shared moral code gains what little persuasion it has from confusion with a quite different one.

There is another point to be noted. It is no doubt true that 'morality', where this means something quite other than a moral code about matters like sexual conduct, is an empirically or even logically necessary condition of the existence of a society. It is true that morality, where this has to do with acceptance of certain principles of mutual tolerance, is a condition of social existence. All societies satisfy some such condition. This is not to say that a particular moral code followed by a society at some point in time is a necessary condition of the society's continuance. There are, of course, other difficulties in the doctrine we are considering. It shares with its predecessor the supposition that there does exist in contemporary society an accepted or shared or established morality of the kind required.

4. *Consent, Culpability, Sincerity*

Although Mill does not succeed in producing a general principle of State intervention, one which does not incorporate the Principle of Utility, his position can be clearly stated. It is that there is to be no intervention unless (1) an individual causes harm, as determined by Utility, to someone other than an agreeing partner, and (2) the harm involves injury to interests sanctioned by Utility. One may be puzzled, at this point, by the inclusion of the second requirement. Why should it not be thought sufficient, as a ground for intervention, simply that an individual causes harm, harm according to the Principle of Utility, to someone not an agreeing partner? I take the argument to be that while an individual may indeed cause harm in the given sense to someone else, to allow the possibility of intervention by the State in *all* such cases would make for an even less acceptable state of affairs. To allow the possibility would so restrict individual freedom as to produce more distress or less satisfaction than the alternative course. The alternative course is to allow the possibility of intervention in some cases. The limit is described by way of the notion of interests. Intervention is a possibility when interests sanctioned by Utility are injured. The doctrine excludes intervention on the ground simply that behaviour is thought to be immoral. Admittedly, the question of whether or not harm is involved is partly an evaluative question which Mill must settle by recourse to his fundamental principle.

We have considered one response to a view of this kind. There are also other criticisms which I should like to consider before making my own, of a rather different kind. One recurring one is that the law, and in particular English and American law, has not followed Mill. It is not in general a defence to establish that the person harmed did in fact consent to the action in question. It is not a defence in cases of assault or euthanasia or suicide pact. The explanation, it is said, of this supposed refusal to countenance the fact of agreeing partners must be that in the law certain acts are punished simply because they are immoral.[26] There are a number of things to be said about this. (1) It is fairly obvious that Mill, when he defended what he called 'the liberty . . . of combination among individuals',[27] did not intend to condemn wholesale the legal principle that the consent of an injured party is not in general a defence. His concern was in the main with 'combinations' of agreeing partners other than those involving such offences as assault and euthanasia. (2) With respect to cases involving such offences, one can reasonably suppose he would have supported such legal rules as have the effect of ensuring that supposed agreements are indeed full agreements between knowledgeable and entirely uncoerced partners. One can also suppose he

26. Devlin, *op. cit.*, p. 132.
27. Mill, *op. cit.*, p. 138.

would have approved of rules whose effect is to ensure that supposed agreements are settled and persistent. Such rules, which do not amount to the prohibition of 'combinations', can hardly be displayed as attempts to punish immorality on the ground alone that it is immorality. They are, rather, strategies to avoid abuse of the liberty of combination, abuse which would consist fundamentally in harm of one individual by another. (3) It must be admitted, despite what has been said, that the law has in the past done more than engage in such strategies. It has punished supposed immorality for itself, and still does so. What can be made of this? Where the given principle of intervention and the law diverge, one can take the law to be mistaken rather than the principle. It is at this point that critics of Mill are wont to have recourse to a supposition about the wisdom of the ages. It is, in one formulation, the supposition 'that there is a presumption that common and long-established institutions are likely to have merits not apparent to the rationalist philosopher'.[28] All that can be said here, since any consideration of what amounts to a considerable ideology is out of question, is that 'common and long-established institutions' come to be taken as indefensible with sufficient regularity to make the present argument less than overwhelming.

There is, it is said,[29] another principle of law which is not at all in accord with Mill's principle. It is clear, we are told, that the law as it stands *takes account of* moral culpability. Offenders are graded in the criminal calendar *partly* in accordance with this consideration; particular offenders are assessed with respect to moral culpability. The law as it stands is not an exemplification of the traditional deterrence theory. It is inconsistent, it is said, to find this morally tolerable and also to maintain that the law may not be used to enforce morality as such. The simplest reply is that even if everything prior to this last proposition is true, there is no such inconsistency. I may with perfect logical respectability, to speak of nothing else, believe (1) that the justification of having a system of punishment and of particular acts of punishment *involves* moral culpability

28. Hart, *Law, Liberty and Morality*, p. 29.
29. Devlin, *op. cit.*, p. 128.

or desert, and (2) that there is no justification for either a system or particular punishments on the ground merely of the supposed immorality of certain behaviour. I shall have to grant, of course, that the law should be 'concerned with morality' where that is understood as a reiteration of the first proposition. This commits me in no way to the view that the law should be 'concerned with morality' where this means there is a justification for punishment in the mere fact of the existence of behaviour thought to be immoral.

We may also notice the objection that individuals who break the law and in so doing offend against accepted morality rarely do so in the conviction that they are right to do so.

> Evidently what Mill visualises is a number of people doing things he himself would disapprove of, but doing them earnestly and openly and after thought and discussion in an endeavour to find the way of life best suited to them as individuals. This seems to me on the whole an idealistic picture. . . . If a free society is better than a disciplined one, it is because—and this certainly was Mill's view— it is better for a man himself that he should be free to seek his own good in his own way and better too for the society to which he belongs, since thereby a way may be found to greater good for all. But no good can come from a man doing what he acknowledges to be evil.[30]

It is easy, it seems, to suppose that a man whose behaviour diverges from one's own morality cannot but acknowledge that he errs. If speculations are to be made in this area, one as good as any is that among homosexuals, individuals who attempt suicide or euthanasia, those who secure abortions or have recourse to prostitutes, very considerable numbers are entirely willing to defend their actions. Of greater importance is the fact that it does not at all follow from a willingness to admit some behaviour is immoral that it is such. It is surely obvious that there does occur in social and moral development, between times when certain behaviour is widely considered

30. *Op. cit.*, pp. 107–8.

immoral and is rare, and times when it is not so considered and is common, other times when it is to some extent engaged in but not widely defended. Finally, as is admitted, it may be argued that those who are sincere and of the opinion that their behaviour is defensible cannot be distinguished from the rest. Given this, it may be maintained that general arguments adduced by Mill for individual freedom should carry the day. In short, whatever evil attaches to insincere behaviour, it is outweighed by the benefits attaching to freedom.

5. *Equality*

As we have noticed, there is a similarity between the retribution theory of punishment and the view, stated at the beginning of the third section above, that an established moral code is of such good *in itself* that we may attempt to maintain it by punishment. They are both in a way anti-utilitarian. Their ends, giving a man what he deserves and maintaining a morality, are such that they pay a quite insufficient attention to welfare. Predictably, then, both doctrines can be rejected.

Mill's thesis, that there is a possibility of State intervention only when there is injury to utility interests, or a danger of it, is closely related to the deterrence theory. Taking only that part of his intervention policy which concerns punishment by the State, it is that a necessary condition of justified punishment is that there be harm of a certain kind, and that supposed immorality is by itself neither a sufficient nor a necessary condition. The latter part rules out the possibility of combination with most forms of the traditional retribution theory. Mill's doctrine does combine with the deterrence theory, in that the necessary condition of justifide punishment is consistent with the sufficient condition proposed by the deterrence theory. Punishment is a possibility, by which I mean that one necessary condition has been satisfied, if behaviour does affect utility interests. Punishment *is* justified, according to the deterrence theory as we have construed it, if this condition is satisfied and it is also true that the punishment is economical.

Mill's doctrine, as we have seen, while it does not fulfil his central intention with respect to a kind of principle, has been the subject of mistaken criticism. It has mistakenly been found inferior to moralistic views which are themselves unacceptable. However, there is at least some criticism against which it cannot be defended. At the end of his essay Mill turns from the subject of intervention in the lives of individuals *against their will* to a different matter: intervention in the form of help, presumably with the agreement of those concerned. He is opposed to it, on the grounds that help is better provided by individuals, that State intervention would here inhibit individual development, that the enlargement of government and bureaucracy, and its power, is a great danger. *A fortiori*, Mill would have been opposed to intervention in the lives of some citizens, against their will, for the purpose of helping others. Almost all contemporary ideologies, although to very differing extents, depart from this attitude. It is worth noticing, incidentally, that at least sometimes such interventions can be regarded as following from Mill's intervention principle. It can in many instances be argued that coercive intervention in the lives of some individuals, in order to make help for others possible, is not against utility interests.

What I wish finally to suggest is that if the state may intervene only if actions harm or threaten utility interests, it will sometimes in its interventions not conform to principles of equality. This will be so, obviously, in several circumstances. Suppose A is claimed to have harmed B. Furthermore, interests of B sanctioned by the Principle of Utility have been injured. There will then be a possibility of intervention given Mill's principle. There is no reason for thinking, however, that the utility interests had by B must be in accordance with equality. The system of interests which includes the relevant interest of B may be such as to maximise utility or welfare. If it preserves unacceptable inequalities between individuals, however, and in particular involves a victimisation of A, there may not be a case for action against A. Consider this over-simplified model. R and S represent the consequences, in terms of quantity of welfare and its distribution, of two possible uses of resources in a society.

Thus, somewhat less welfare would be produced by the first possible use, but its distribution would be into equal shares for three parties concerned, A and B being two of them. The second use would produce more welfare, but its distribution necessarily would be into large shares for B and C and one very small share for A. His share would not only be greatly

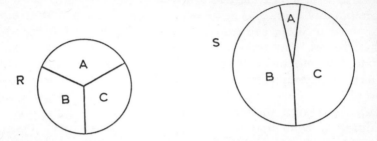

smaller than the other two, given the second possible use of resources, but would also be considerably smaller than the share he would receive given the first possible use. The Principle of Utility requires that the society make the second use of the resources. Suppose now that the society acts on this principle and interests are established in accordance with it. In particular it adopts the second use of resources, which involves the unequal distribution and what amounts to victimisation of A. Suppose that A attempts in a certain way to appropriate a part of B's share. In doing so, he endangers the utility interests of B. According to the intervention principle, there may then be action against him. This may be unacceptable, and clearly so in certain circumstances. There is the circumstance, for example, where each of the three parties requires a share of the sizes in R in order to come up to some agreed minimum standard of welfare.

I am aware that this is excessively schematic and that it avoids a great deal of complication and argument.[31] For obvious reasons, I shall not attempt to say more. My conclusion is that an acceptable principle of State intervention must

31. See, for some of it, Nicholas Rescher, *Distributive Justice* (New York, 1966).

accommodate not only utilitarian values but also equality. It seems clear, although not fully argued here, that it cannot be established that to accommodate the first is invariably to accommodate the second. The deterrence theory of punishment, and the associated doctrine of State intervention, fail in being merely utilitarian. We are left with only the possibilities of a certain compromise theory of punishment and an intervention policy that is similar in that it observes considerations both of utility and equality.

One may have a certain amount of difficulty, at this point, in getting these several questions and their relation into focus. Mill set out to establish one necessary condition of justified intervention by the State or society in the lives of individuals against their wills. If we set aside part of his concern, having to do with coercion by other means than punishment, his problem can be put in either of these two ways: When is punishment *not* justified? or What is one necessary condition of justified punishment? His answer, as we have concluded, putting it in terms of the second formulation, is that a necessary but not sufficient condition of justified punishment is that an individual have injured or endangered the utility interests of someone else, not an agreeing partner. Our main question in the preceding chapters has been this one: What, if anything, constitutes a sufficient condition of justified punishment? One answer is that punishment's being economically deterrent, and that alone, is a sufficient condition. As I have said, these two answers to our question are consistent. One can go further, I think, preferably on the basis of more detailed argument than I shall supply. It can be argued that to answer the second question in this way commits one to answering the first question in Mill's way. One is committed, certainly, to giving a necessary condition of justified punishment that it be deterrent. To maintain that punishment must be deterrent is ordinarily to maintain that it must prevent certain possible distress. This is the same distress, presumably, that is to be avoided by a respect of utility interests and intervention to prevent their injury.

We have rejected Mill's answer to his question, and concluded instead that punishment must not be in question if there is no injury or danger to interests established on the basis of both utility and equality. Such injury or danger is a necessary condition of justified punishment. To the question of a sufficient condition of justified punishment, we have answered that punishment may be justified when it is both economically deterrent and in a certain accord with equality. Again, the second answer is consistent with the first. Again, I wish to suggest, the second answer entail scertain answers to the first question. We must give as one necessary condition of justified punishment that it be deterrent and in accord with equality.[32] This is, it seems, tantamount to the claim that punishment must not be in question if there is no danger or injury to interests established on the basis of utility and equality.

Given a certain concern we need never ask the first question. We need never ask it if our business is with the whole justification of the practice of punishment. We may find ourselves asking it if, in a way like Mill, we face a certain challenge. It is the challenge that one of what we take to be necessary conditions of justified punishment is not such.

32. Also a possibility, of course, is that we give as a necessary condition of justified punishment either that it be deterrent or that it observe equality in a certain way.

Index